GERTIE SEWS JIFFY DRESSES

A MODERN GUIDE TO STITCH-AND-WEAR VINTAGE PATTERNS YOU CAN MAKE IN A DAY

GRETCHEN HIRSCH

Photographs by
SHAMELESS PHOTOGRAPHY (ANGELA ALTUS)

Illustrations by
GEMINI.H

Technical illustrations by
ROBIN KATAJA-BLAIR

ABRAMS • NEW YORK

Contents

Introduction

Over the years, I've become known for my obsession with advanced sewing techniques, taking my cues from the vintage dressmaking books I adore so much. I've espoused a love of complicated tailoring and spent hours pad-stitching lapels. I've become so acquainted with finely engineered strapless bodices that I could probably steel-bone a princess seam in my sleep. But as I started traveling and teaching more (with less time at home for sewing), I also became a devotee of a sort of guilty pleasure: the quick and easy dress. The kind of dress that you can cut out in the morning and wear on a date in the evening. Made of cheerful floral cottons, these dresses are quick and satisfying to sew, and even more fun to wear. Some of my easiest projects to sew have become staples in my wardrobe because of their low maintenance for everyday life. Everyone loves a sew-and-wear dress!

This sort of project is certainly not at odds with a vintage aesthetic. Women have always struggled to fit their love of sewing into their busy lifestyles, and the commercially available patterns of the 1950s and early '60s reflect this. Arguably the most famous home sewing pattern of all time is Butterick's 1952 "Walkaway Dress," a frock so simple that you could sew it up in the morning and "walk away" wearing it to a luncheon. In the '50s and '60s, Simplicity published its popular line of "Jiffy" sewing patterns, which had minimal pattern pieces and simple construction yet were still chic enough to appeal to a fashion-conscious customer. These ideas appeal now more than ever to novice and experienced seamstresses alike.

But while I love a project that comes together almost effortlessly, I also feel conflicted about how the DIY movement has become overtaken with fast and easy projects. Fabric stores advertise "no sew" projects, and real skill has been eschewed for speed. Ultimately, I think the obsession with "quick and easy" has made us lose touch with why we wanted to start sewing in the first place: to slow down, to have tactile experiences, to take pride in a learned skill.

So why write this book? Because I want to show that it's possible to cultivate real sewing skills without spending days or even weeks on a project. Sewing more projects means more practice! I always like to tell my students how I didn't become truly skilled at lapped zippers until I sewed twenty-five of them in a row for my last book, *Gertie's Ultimate Dress Book*. Making lots of easy dresses will certainly make you a better sewer, especially if you repeat fundamental skills (like bindings, setting in sleeves, and zippers) to the point that you build muscle memory. If you're just learning, practice the dresses in this book and then challenge yourself with something more complicated (my previous books and my Charm Patterns line, for instance!).

If you are already a confident seamstress, then I hope the vintage aesthetic of the projects in this book will still appeal to you. It was important to me to design these patterns so that they could stand on their own as great examples of retro fashion, without necessarily advertising the fact that they weren't that difficult to make. I was endlessly inspired by '50s-era designer Claire McCardell while designing the patterns. Her work was living proof that complicated doesn't necessarily equal chic, and that the simplest of garments can be a revelation.

Another question you may be asking is, why all dresses? Most vintage-loving ladies say dresses are their favorite thing to sew and to wear, and I enthusiastically agree. Even after devoting an entire book to the subject of dresses and several years to teaching dressmaking workshops based

The Patio Dress (page 127)

The Patio Dress with Short Sleeves (page 133)

on that material, I don't feel done with dresses. Quite the opposite! I'm endlessly fascinated by frocks, and I became enamored of the challenge of creating a library of easy dress designs that were also quite stylish.

INSIDE THE BOOK

In part one, you will discover the skills you need to make lovely dresses: from choosing and cutting fabric to functional and decorative finishing touches. You'll also learn fitting techniques and some simple patternmaking to customize your dress wardrobe. Part two is a collection of dresses made from the five included patterns (see the envelope in the back). I show variations on each pattern as well, to illustrate that with a little ingenuity you can make one pattern multiple times with a dazzling array of results!

No matter your prior experience, I hope this book will help you discover (or rediscover!) a love of dressmaking. And I especially hope that it will remind you that sewing doesn't have to be laborious or painstaking to be satisfying and beautiful.

PART ONE

CHAPTER ONE

Supplies and Tools

This chapter is your bible for setting the scene to sew. Start with befriending your sewing machine! It's your faithful sidekick on the road to a beautiful wardrobe of dresses. Next, we'll take a look at the rest of the cast of characters: all the supplies and tools you'll need to have handy in order to sew skillfully.

Sewing Machines

All you really need in a sewing machine is a good straight stitch, a zigzag, and a buttonhole. That's why I sew on a basic, all-metal mechanical machine with very few features; I just don't like a lot of extras. You probably have a relative with an old machine like this that just needs a good servicing! The old '70s Singer that I learned to sew on as a little girl is a fantastic machine, but I see people get rid of that style all the time, thinking they're outdated and better replaced with a new computerized machine. The truth is these old metal mechanical machines are great starter setups: easy to understand and with just the right amount of features.

The best thing you can do for your dressmaking is to really get to know your sewing machine. Read through the manual, and then spend a little time threading and rethreading it and then sewing long pieces of fabric. Practice sewing with a ⅝" (1.5 cm) seam allowance by

Correct hand position

aligning the edge of the fabric with the correct line on the metal needle plate—that's the seam allowance that most garment patterns use (including the patterns in this book). Being able to keep a consistent seam allowance is one of the most important machine-sewing skills. If you're even ⅛" (3 mm) off on each side seam of a dress, that adds up to your garment being ½" (1.3 cm) smaller or bigger than you planned. And that can make a huge difference in a fitted bodice! I always remind my beginner students to look at the seam allowance guide as they sew, not the needle.

Hand position is also very important. Don't push or pull the fabric through the machine—that's what the feed dogs are for (feed dogs are the ridged bars attached to gears under the presser foot that pull the fabric through). Sometimes you may need to hold the fabric taut from front and back to avoid puckers in your sewing, but the machine will do the rest of the work. Your left hand gently rests on top of the fabric to guide it (remember to watch that ⅝" [1.5 cm] seam allowance guide on the needle plate) and your right hand loosely holds the fabric in front of the machine. You can angle your hand slightly upward to keep the fabric taut.

If you're a newbie, spend a little time mastering accurate seam allowances and your machine sewing technique, and the rest will be much easier!

MACHINE SUPPLIES AND ACCESSORIES

Here are the basic supplies to go with your machine.

- **NEEDLES:** Machine needles come in different sizes and types, and you need to use the right kind for your fabric. I use three sizes of needles: size 70/10 for thin fabrics, size 80/12 for medium-weight fabrics, and

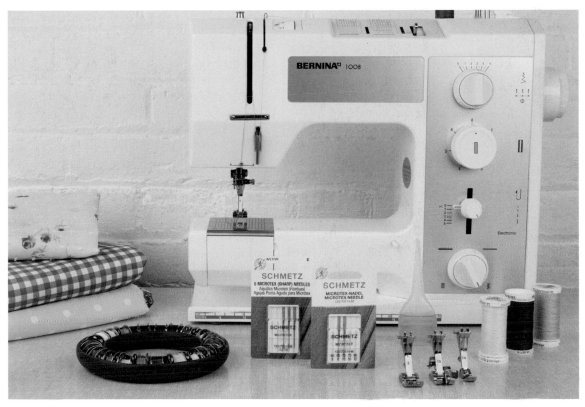

MACHINE AND ACCESSORIES (clockwise from left): bobbins in case, basic sewing machine, thread, sewing machine feet, sewing machine oil, sewing machine needles

size 90/14 for thick fabrics. (Note that the higher the number is, the thicker the needle.) As for needle type, I like microtex for their sharp point. Other types you should know about are ballpoint (for jersey and stretch fabrics) and universal (which work on a variety of fabrics). For the projects in this book, use either microtex or universal needles. And don't forget to change the needle every few projects; they get dull with wear, compromising your stitch quality and leading to breakage.

- **BOBBINS:** Have plenty of empty bobbins around, and make sure they're the same class that came with your machine. You don't have to use brand-name bobbins (those are often more expensive without actually being a better product), but bring a bobbin from your machine to the store to compare size

and shape. Use metal bobbins if your machine came with metal, and plastic bobbins if it came with plastic.

- **OIL:** Check your machine's manual to see if it needs to be oiled regularly (some are self-lubricating). If it does, make sure to oil it every few projects to keep it running smoothly. Take out the bobbin case and squeeze two drops of oil into the shuttle (that's what the bobbin case fits into). With no needle in the machine, press the foot pedal to run the machine for a few seconds. Finally, put some scrap fabric into the machine and feed it through (still with no needle) to absorb any of the oil, so you don't get it on your next dress!
- **TWEEZERS:** Good to have around if you need to pull any stray threads or lint out of the machine.

Basic Presser Feet

Your machine should have come with a variety of presser feet (the part that clamps down and holds the fabric flat as it's stitched), but you can always order them if you're missing any. Here are the absolute essentials:

- **BASIC/ZIGZAG:** This is the foot that will be on your machine most of the time. It's the default presser foot and will work with both a straight stitch and a zigzag, as well as a variety of decorative stitches.
- **ZIPPER:** For the projects in this book, you'll need only a regular (not invisible) zipper foot. It allows you to stitch on either side of the zipper teeth, without stitching over them.
- **BLIND HEM/EDGESTITCH:** I have an edgestitch foot that I love, and a blind hem foot can serve the same function. An edgestitch foot is just a simple presser foot with a dull "blade" that runs up the middle. To use it, set the needle to stitch on one side of the blade or the other, and then align the blade with a seam or fabric fold so that you can stitch on either side consistently. It's great for things like understitching, where you need to stitch very close to a seamline. It's also fabulous for

THE SERGER

A serger is a machine that trims your fabric with a blade and neatly finishes the edges with an overlock stitch (look inside most any store-bought garment to see an example!). It has many uses, including seaming knit fabrics and neatly finishing the raw edges of your seam allowances. Do you need a serger for basic dressmaking? Absolutely not! Is it nice to have? Hell, yes! I generally finish all my seams on my serger, and that's all I do with it. Considering there are lots of other ways to finish seams (see pages 40–41), it's definitely more of a convenience than a necessity. That said, I adore my serger. I sew a lot of dresses, so it's important to me to be able to quickly and professionally finish seams.

When using my serger to finish seams, I always do the majority of this step right after cutting and marking (see chapter three), and

Serging as an edge finish

before stitching any seams (so I'm only serging through one layer). Serge the edges of any side seams, shoulder seams, and pockets, being careful not to trim away any fabric. You can always disengage the serger's blade if that helps you avoid cutting any fabric.

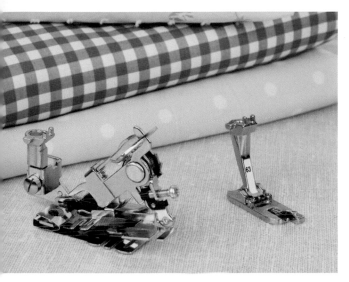

The ruffler and presser foot

fabulous tiered ruffles. See page 42 for detailed information on using them.

- **RUFFLER FOOT:** This is a crazy-looking contraption that makes little pleats on fabric, creating the effect of ruffles.
- **NARROW HEMMER:** This foot creates a narrow double hem quickly, making it the perfect companion to the ruffler foot. Use the narrow hemmer to make a quick hem on yards and yards of ruffles in a snap! It's a little tricky to get the hang of, but once you've practiced a bit you'll be amazed at how quickly it makes a lovely little hem.

stitching on pockets, so you get a nice even topstitch all the way around. (You'll learn more about these types of stitches in chapter four.) You can use the blind hem foot (which most likely came with your machine) for the same purpose, since it also has a blade down the center of the foot. Use it in the same way as the edgestitch foot by positioning the needle on one side of the blade or the other.

- **BUTTONHOLE:** You need a special foot for making buttonholes, and it should have come with your machine. If your machine makes an automatic (or "one-step") buttonhole, your buttonhole foot will have a place to insert a button, ensuring that each buttonhole comes out the right size. For old-school mechanical machines (like the one I use), the buttonhole foot will be very similar to the basic foot but will have grooves in the bottom so the raised buttonhole can slide under it without catching. (Read more about making buttonholes on page 54.)

OPTIONAL SPECIAL PRESSER FEET

Some of the dress variations in this book include the use of the following two presser feet to create

MACHINE DOS AND DON'TS

Machine DON'TS

- Never turn the handwheel (also called a "balance wheel") away from you, only toward you (counterclockwise). Turning it in the wrong direction can harm the motor.
- Don't pull the upper thread up out of the machine. Cut it off near the spool, and then pull the cut thread down and out through the needle. This eliminates lint and potential machine problems down the road.
- Don't sew without fabric under the presser foot. It can cause knotting and other issues.

Machine DOS

- Use the correct needle size and type, and always change it every couple of projects (don't just wait for it to break!).
- Oil your machine regularly if it is not self-lubricating (see page 11).
- Take it in for regular servicing, about once a year.

Machine Troubleshooting

Don't let machine issues keep you from your sewing dreams! After teaching sewing for many years, here are the most common problems I see. If anything funky is happening with your machine, check this list before taking it in for servicing.

- Is the presser foot down? (Sorry, I had to ask!) If you're new to sewing, this is a mistake you'll make a lot. Pretty soon it will be second nature to put it down every time, I promise.

- Is the upper thread correctly threaded into the take-up lever? The most common issue I see with beginner sewers is that the thread is not in the hole of the take-up lever (that silver apparatus on the front of the machine that goes up and down as you stitch). If the thread isn't actually inserted into the hole in the lever, you will get a crazy nest of thread on the back of your fabric.

- Is the needle hitting something when it goes down? This means your bobbin case isn't clicked all the way into its position.

- Is the bobbin inserted into the case properly (for front-loading bobbins)? The tail of thread should be coming off the bobbin in a P shape, not a Q shape. Remember: P for perfect!

- Is the bobbin wound correctly? When you squeeze the sides of the bobbin, the thread should not feel squishy. It should be uniformly wound, with no loose threads.

- Is the upper thread coming unthreaded when you start to sew? This means that you didn't have the needle all the way up when you removed the fabric at the end of your last seam. Before you take the fabric out from under the presser foot, turn the handwheel toward you until the take-up lever is at its highest position.

- Are the stitches too loose or tight? Loose stitches look like loops and don't lay flat on the fabric, and tight stitches pull, creating ripples in the fabric. This points to a tension issue. Consult your manual for adjustments. If the stitches on the wrong side of the fabric are loose or tight, adjust the upper thread tension. If the stitches on the right side of the fabric are loose or tight, adjust the bobbin tension.

Ironing Equipment

For a polished finish, it's crucial to press your dress as you sew it. For instance, you need to press each seam after you sew it; the projects in part two will give you pressing instructions as necessary. Here's what you'll need for proper pressing.

- **STEAM IRON:** Buy a good basic iron. Unfortunately, most irons on the market seem to stop working after a while and start leaking. I've tried the fanciest irons money can buy, but I keep coming back to the Black and Decker Digital Advantage iron, which I replace every couple of years.

- **FULL-SIZE IRONING BOARD:** You need a good-size, stable surface for pressing dresses as you sew them.

- **PRESS CLOTH:** I love sheer organza press cloths (Dritz sells them, or you can buy 100 percent silk organza—not polyester—and pink or serge the edges) because you can see through them. You'll want to use the press cloth between the iron and the fabric when applying fusible interfacing (see page 34), or when pressing a fabric that is subject to heat damage, like wool, synthetic, or metallic fabric.

PRESSING EQUIPMENT: iron, organza press cloth, tailor's ham, spray bottle

- **WATER SPRAY BOTTLE:** This is good to have for dampening interfacing before applying the iron, and it can help to remove stubborn wrinkles.
- **TAILOR'S HAM:** Please don't try to sew a dart without one of these! This is a stuffed pressing tool in the shape of the meat product it's named for. It's a firm, curved surface for pressing areas of a garment that aren't flat, like a dart or a hip curve. Trying to press these areas on a flat surface will result in ripples and creases. Place the curved area of the garment over one of the curved areas of the ham, but do not stretch the fabric; this may cause fabric distortion and weird bubbling when the garment is worn. Press the iron on the ham.

Your Basic Sewing Kit

I'm always a little surprised by the low-quality supplies that I see people sew with: enormous plastic-head pins that melt and leave holes in fabric, dull paper scissors to hack away at fabric, linty dollar-bin thread that breaks. It's so much more enjoyable to use the right materials! I know it can take a while to build up a good arsenal, but sometimes the good stuff only costs a little bit more. You just have to know where to find it! So here I write very specifically about the brands I use, not as part of any official endorsement, but so that you know exactly what to look for when seeking out better-quality supplies. Keep in mind that you might need to order online.

- **THREAD:** All-purpose polyester thread is what you want for garments, for both the machine and hand-sewing. I use Gütermann or Mettler brands, but as long as it's not the super cheap stuff (or really old), it should be fine to sew with. Have a bunch of colors at the ready.
- **FABRIC SHEARS:** You'll need a good, sharp pair of scissors that are only for cutting out fabric. My favorite is Kai 5230, 9"- (23 cm-) long scissors with a bent handle that makes cutting flat fabric easier. I go for a plastic handle because I find it lighter in weight and easier on my wrists for long cutting sessions. Have your shears sharpened about once a year

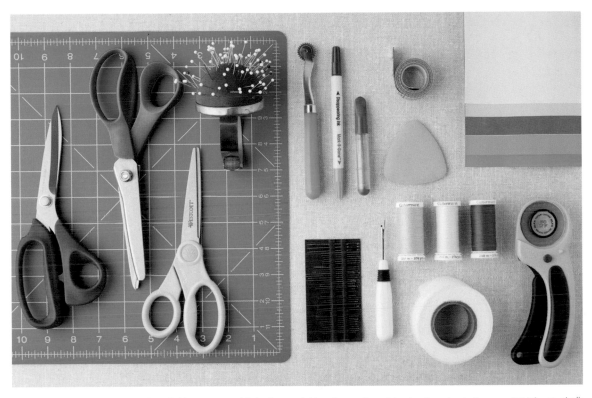

BASIC SEWING KIT (clockwise from left): rotary mat, fabric shears, pinking shears, pincushion, tracing wheel, disappearing ink pen, chalk pen, chalk, tape measure, tracing paper, rotary cutter, thread, fusible stay tape, seam ripper, hand sewing needles, paper scissors

(or whenever they get dull). Kai and Gingher both have mail-in sharpening for their scissors, and your local fabric store or cooking supply shop can recommend a place that sharpens shears and knives. Try your local hardware store; they may be able to do it there!

- **PAPER SCISSORS:** Any pair of craft or office scissors will do; these are for cutting out pattern paper. Using your fabric shears on paper will dull them faster than usual, so you want to keep these two separate scissors for their distinct purposes.

- **PINKING SHEARS:** A good option for finishing seams if you don't have a serger. You don't need to buy anything expensive, as they don't seem to vary too much in quality and usually need to be replaced every few years.

- **PINS:** Buy quality glass-head pins! My favorites are Clover silk pins, with the red and white glass heads. Silk pins are strong and very sharp, yet they are small enough that they won't pierce large holes in your fabric.

- **PINCUSHION:** I could never be without my Bohin wrist pincushion. It's so pretty, like a bracelet! The band is adjustable and I wear it a few inches up from my wrist for easy access while I'm at the sewing machine taking out pins. If you don't like wrist cushions, the classic tomato pincushion or a magnetic dish work well, too.

- **HAND-SEWING NEEDLES:** I'm not very picky about hand-sewing needles; a multipack of sharps with various sizes will do just fine.

- **ROTARY CUTTER AND MAT:** A rotary cutter looks like a pizza cutter with a very sharp blade, and it's used on top of a special self-healing mat. If you have a large enough mat, you can use your rotary cutter for cutting out entire dresses. I generally use mine for cutting out bias strips (see page 48), because it's great for using against a clear ruler to cut long straight lines. I also love it for getting a clean cut on knit interfacing, which can sometimes be tricky to cut with shears. A rotary cutter can be great for difficult fabrics in general, because the fabric remains flat on the table and doesn't shift as you're cutting it.

- **MARKING SUPPLIES:** You'll need something to transfer darts and pattern symbols onto fabric. Keep several marking options on hand for different fabrics and purposes.

  — **Chalk pens:** I love Clover Chaco Liners; they dispense a thin line of chalk that is very visible on fabric. Have a couple of colors on hand (pink and white are my go-to colors) for different tones of fabric.

  — **Invisible marking pens:** I like Dritz's Dual Purpose Marking Pen; it has a purple side with disappearing ink (it fades after about twenty-four hours) and a blue side with ink that washes out. I especially like the purple side, as it shows up very well on light-colored fabrics.

  — **Dressmaker's tracing paper:** This is a coated paper that comes in different colors and is used with a tracing wheel to copy marks onto fabric. I especially like the big sheets of wax-coated paper (see Resources, page 138), but they are hard to find and the wax doesn't really come out of fabric, so you have to be sure you use a color that doesn't show on the right side. Because of the limitations of wax paper, I make sure to have chalk-coated paper as well: Saral and Clover make versions of this. It washes out easily but leaves a very faint line in most cases.

- **SEAM RIPPER:** A girl's best friend for fixing sewing mistakes and removing other unwanted stitches like basting (long machine or hand stitches that hold fabric together temporarily). Find one with a small and very sharp point; I love my Clover seam ripper. The easiest way to remove a row of stitches is to use the blade of the seam ripper to cut the thread about every three stitches, holding the fabric flat. On the other side of the fabric, pull the thread; it should come out in one long piece. Then pull the two pieces of fabric apart and clean up any remaining small thread pieces.

- **TRACING WHEEL:** Get the kind with the spoked wheel to use with dressmaker's tracing paper to copy darts and other pattern markings.

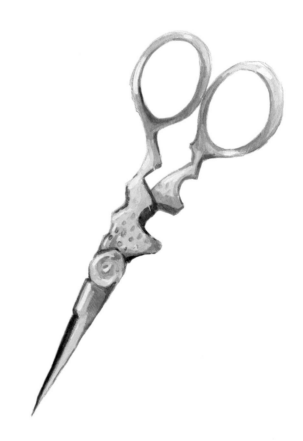

Other Supplies

These are things you'll need for tracing patterns, testing the fit, and making any changes on paper.

- **PATTERN PAPER OR TRACING PAPER:** You'll need paper to trace the patterns in this book, as well as to make any fitting or design changes. I order big rolls of fashion pattern paper (see Resources, page 138), but you can also use any large paper on a roll, like art tracing paper or butcher paper. See my methods for tracing patterns on page 30. Swedish tracing paper is pricey, but it is a good option for tissue fitting (a quick fitting done by pinning the tissue together and checking it on your body), as it behaves like fabric (you can even sew it, if you like).
- **MUSLIN:** Always keep some muslin fabric at the ready to test patterns (Brits and Aussies know this fabric as "calico"). Making a muslin mock-up is an important part of testing the fit of a pattern (see page 73).
- **RULER:** A 2" x 18" (5 cm x 46 cm) clear gridded ruler is one of the tools I reach for most when it comes to tracing patterns, making fit changes, and adding seam allowances to patterns (only if needed; the patterns in this book already include seam allowances).
- **FRENCH CURVE OR CURVED RULER:** This helps you trace curved pattern pieces and draw in curved seam allowances and new necklines.
- **VARIOUS PENCILS:** I like mechanical pencils for tracing patterns, and then I like to have colored pencils handy to make changes to patterns.
- **TRANSPARENT TAPE:** For pattern changes; also doubles as a weight to hold down your patterns on your fabric if you get the heavy dispenser!

CHAPTER TWO

Fabrics

One of the most difficult (and exciting!) parts of starting to sew dresses is figuring out how to match the right fabric with a pattern. Learning a bit about some easy-to-sew fabrics will go a long way in reducing confusion on the topic. In this chapter, I'll describe some of my favorite dressmaking fabrics, give a primer on key fabric terms, and write a bit about the different trims that can elevate your dresses to something truly unique!

Here are some of my favorite fabrics for simple dressmaking projects. Fabric has both a fiber and a type (which usually refers to its weave), so you'll typically see fabric described with two words, like "cotton voile" or "wool crepe." I've divided these sections by fiber, but there are many subcategories of fabric type within these fibers. To keep things simple, I'm only going over easy-to-sew fabrics, but keep in mind that there's a whole wide, wonderful world of more exotic dressmaking fabrics out there.

Fabric Glossary

WOVEN: A type of fabric that produces a stable material, like a quilting cotton. In a woven fabric, threads or yarns weave over and under each other in a variety of ways. All the projects in this book were designed for woven fabrics (as opposed to knits, which require different fitting and construction skills). Woven fibers vary greatly in weight, type of weave, and drape, but they all have a warp (the grain or direction that runs parallel to the selvage [the tightly woven finished edges of the fabric]) and a weft (the grain that is perpendicular to the selvage). Some can include spandex for stretch, usually incorporated in the crosswise grain, best oriented to go around the body.

KNIT: In contrast to woven fabrics, the knit process of looping yarns around each other produces a fabric with stretch, like jersey (think T-shirts and yoga pants). Because knit fabrics behave much differently from wovens, sewing patterns are generally designed specifically for knits (or specifically for wovens). Knits, except for very stable, nonstretch varieties, like some double knits, are not a good choice for the projects in this book.

HAND: A fabric's hand refers to its feel. Think of how a length of fabric feels to the touch; it may be soft and plush like velvet, stiff like organza, liquid like charmeuse, or even crunchy like taffeta!

DRAPE: A fabric with drape falls in soft, fluid folds and flows smoothly over the body rather than standing away from it. Fabrics known for having good drape are rayon challis, silk crepe, and cotton voile.

BODY: The opposite of drape; fabrics with body fall in stiff cones and do not naturally cling to the figure. They hold shape well, making them perfect for '50s-style silhouettes with structured bodices and full skirts. Sateen, poplin, and broadcloth are examples of fabric with body.

Cotton

I always go to cotton first for an easy day dress! It's so comfortable to wear, is easy to sew, and needs minimal care. Here are a few of my favorite types of cotton fabrics.

BROADCLOTH/QUILTING COTTONS: If you're making your first dress, this is a great starter fabric. It's a very stable, easy-to-sew fabric that comes in every solid shade of the rainbow and in countless prints, ranging from understated to the wackiest novelty prints you can dream of. Good-quality quilting cottons can work for garments, as they tend to have a nice drape (halfway between fluid and stiff) and a soft, dry hand. Avoid anything too stiff. The Popover Dress on page 84 was made from an inexpensive quilting cotton, and the fabric's body worked well for the A-line silhouette.

LAWN/BATISTE/VOILE: These are three similar types of lightweight and smooth-textured cottons that work well for warm-weather dresses. Lawn is a lovely cotton, the most famous brand of which is Liberty of London, with its amazing prints

(my favorite of all time is Liberty Carline, a '50s rose print, seen made up in the Patio Dress on page 133). Batiste is a lightweight, semiopaque cotton that mostly comes in solids; it is often used for heirloom children's garments but would also make beautiful women's dresses. Voile is the lightest of the three and can be very sheer, so it may require a lining or underlining or a slip underneath.

DOTTED SWISS: A sweetly textured cotton with little raised tufts or embroidered dots. It can be on the sheer side and works nicely for summer dresses.

SATEEN: This is a crisp fabric with a satiny sheen that can be either subtle or more noticeable. It's generally opaque, so it doesn't necessarily require a lining and would be a great choice for most of the projects in this book. See the border print Swirl Dress on page 104 for an example of a dress made in sateen.

EYELET: This is a beautiful cotton fabric with decorative holes that are embroidered all the way around. It has a casual and sweet vibe, and comes in a ton of colors. Eyelet usually requires a lining or underlining, or you can go vintage chic and wear a pretty slip underneath. Sometimes eyelet fabrics have pretty scalloped selvages, too.

GAUZE/DOUBLE GAUZE: This is a fabric that feels so soft and wonderful against the skin! It is light and airy because of its loose weave, meaning it can be sheer. Japanese double gauzes (which have two layers joined together) tend to have more opacity and would be a great choice for casual day dresses.

GINGHAM: A fabric beloved by vintage enthusiasts and, well, everybody! Gingham has checks (ranging from delicate in size to enormous) in two colors that are woven into the fabric. If you're a novice sewer, I recommend choosing checks that are ¼" (6 mm) or less, as they're small enough that you don't need to worry about matching them at the seams.

PIQUÉ: A textured fabric with a waffle-like surface that comes in various weights and lots of colors. It's great for simple dressmaking projects, as it tends to be more on the opaque side and doesn't require a lining.

Other Fabric Fibers

Besides cotton, there are other fibers you can use to sew easy dresses. Here are a few:

LINEN: Linen is a beautiful natural plant fiber that is known for its comfort and breathability. Unfortunately, it's also known for its tendency to wrinkle and crease. Linen-and-rayon-blend fabrics have a very nice drape and tend to wrinkle a bit less than 100-percent linen fabrics (I used one on the Square Neckline variation on the Chemise Dress on page 101). Linen looks very pretty in summer dresses, especially if you just ignore the creasing and embrace the relaxed vibe!

RAYON: This is a fiber derived from wood pulp (cellulose) and it comes in different

weaves, such as challis, twill, and crepe. It's one of my favorites for dresses that benefit from excellent drape. For instance, the Chemise Dress (page 95) looks best in a fabric that skims over the body rather than standing away from it, so rayon challis is a perfect choice. Rayon challis, twill, and crepe are all lovely for this type of dress. I prefer to hand-wash rayon, as it can pill and shrink in the machine.

WOOL: This is a lovely natural fiber associated with cozy cool-weather garments. I tend to reserve wool for more complex dressmaking projects, as it definitely benefits from a lining. However, some wools are not scratchy; some wool crepes are soft against the skin, so you may wish to explore wool crepe for a simple day dress. Wool requires some thought and care: Before sewing you should preshrink it by steaming with an iron, and it's a good idea to always use a press cloth to avoid leaving shiny spots.

SILK: This fiber definitely works best for more involved and dressier sewing projects. If you'd like to sew with silk, start by exploring fabrics with body that aren't too difficult to sew, like shantung, dupioni, or tweed. These would work well in more structured silhouettes like the Boatneck Dress on page 112. (In fact, I used a double-faced stretch silk mikado for the bodice of the Boatneck party dress variation on page 123.)

General Categories of Fabric

These are a few types of fabric that are not confined to a particular fiber but are important to know about.

EMBROIDERED FABRICS AND BORDER PRINTS: One of my favorite fabrics to sew with (and design) is anything with a beautiful border. By this I mean anything from an eyelet with a scalloped selvage to a true border-print fabric. A border print has a design that runs along the selvage, like my rose prints pictured here. Border prints and embroidered selvages can be used along the bottom of a skirt like the Swirl Dress on page 104 or the Boatneck Dress on page 112. Just position the border along the hemline of the dress when cutting out the skirt. Keep in mind that this type of placement is best for skirts that have straight rather than curved hems; for example, the extreme curve of a circle skirt hem doesn't follow the straight line of a border along a fabric's selvage.

Border-print and scalloped-edge fabrics

PLAIDS, STRIPES, AND CHECKS: I love this category! However, these fabrics are known for being tricky to sew since they require a plan and lots of care for matching them up across seamlines, and they sometimes require extra fabric. For instance, on the side seam of a skirt, it's a good idea to match the lines or squares of a plaid, striped, or checked pattern so that they

continue across the seam without a break or jog. It takes careful fabric layout to ensure that a stripe appears at the same point on the front and back of a garment piece. You'll need to align the stripe to the same position along the seams on the front and back pattern pieces before carefully cutting. This may require cutting the fabric in a single layer rather than doubled. You can also match lines of a plaid on the bias, like I did for the Bias Variation on the Popover Dress on page 90, where the gingham meets up in a V-shape at the center front. Another fun trick with these fabrics is to cut certain pieces on the bias, like I did for the pockets and waist tie on the Swirl Dress variation on page 111.

NAPPED AND DIRECTIONAL PRINT FABRICS: Fabrics with nap include velvet, velour, and corduroy. The "nap" or "pile" is the texture of the fabric, the way it's formed with a short coat of threads that stand up on end like an animal's fur. Just like a cat's fur, the nap lies better in one direction than the other (think of petting the cat's fur in either direction: one way is smooth and the other way is not). Napped fabrics need to be cut so that the nap all goes in one direction, so you may need extra fabric for your cutting layout. Don't worry too much about napped fabrics if you're a novice dressmaker, but you may run into a related type of fabric: the directional print. This means that a print is meant to go in one direction only (usually up or down). Think of a cute novelty print like flamingos standing up, all in the same direction.

You wouldn't want to cut a dress out of that fabric with the flamingos facing upside down! So, much like a napped fabric, you must cut all the pieces so that the flamingos are facing the right way. Again, this may require some tweaking of the cutting layout and purchasing a bit more fabric. Additionally, if you had planned to cut a rectangular gathered skirt along the selvage of the fabric (as for the Boatneck Dress on page 112), it may not work, as the flamingos may end up facing sideways. Instead, you may need to cut the fabric across the width of the yardage and create a seam at center front, if needed, to gain more fabric width.

Fabric Care

Some fabrics need to be prewashed before sewing to avoid shrinkage after you've already sewn your dress (this could be quite distressing!). Washing your yardage can also help soften the fabric's hand by removing some of the fiber coatings that are applied in the manufacturing process, as well as other residues from manufacturing, shipping, and store display.

For most of the cotton dresses in this book, I machine-washed the fabric first. Then I either machine-dried it, for a sturdy fabric like quilting cotton, or hung it to line-dry, for more delicate weaves like the tweed for the Boatneck Dress sheath variation (page 119).

When it comes to more delicate fabrics like rayon, silk, and tulle, hand-washing or dry-cleaning is best. In this case, I usually skip the prewashing. However, if you are concerned about your fabric shrinking, hand-wash the yardage and hang it to dry. (I love to use lingerie wash or special liquid soap like Soak for hand-washing, as it doesn't need to be rinsed out.) Press if needed.

The Patio Dress with Short Sleeves (page 133)

CHAPTER THREE

Getting Ready to Sew

This chapter is about all the things you do before you sit at the sewing machine: tracing your patterns, laying out your fabric, cutting out the pieces, transferring any marks from the pattern to the fabric, and applying interfacing (a fusible material used to add body to fabric). Moving efficiently through these steps means you can get to the sewing part faster! While it may be tempting to leave steps for later (like dealing with fusible interfacing), it's always a good idea to get this prep work out of the way so you can enjoy your time at the machine without interruption.

Pattern Tracing

SUPPLIES FOR PATTERN TRACING

Some of my most-used tracing supplies should already be a part of your basic sewing kit: pattern paper, tracing wheel, a gridded clear ruler, a French curve, and regular and colored pencils (see pages 16–19). Aside from the those usual supplies, there are a couple of additional tools you'll want specifically for tracing patterns and making pattern changes.

- **CORKBOARD**: I like to use this as my surface when tracing patterns. When you use a tracing wheel on top of corkboard, it creates little perforations in the pattern paper that you can use as a guide to pencil in the pattern outlines.
- **MUSLIN/CALICO**: Once you've traced the pattern, it's always a good idea to cut out the pieces (at least the bodice) in muslin fabric and sew it up to test the fit. The best kind of muslin to get for this purpose is medium weight, and it's always good to have on hand!

SUPPLIES FOR PATTERN TRACING (clockwise from upper left): muslin, tape, yardstick, clear ruler, colored pencils, mechanical pencil, French curve, tracing wheel, corkboard

TRACING YOUR PATTERNS

Some patterns you might buy don't necessarily need to be traced, like commercial patterns printed on tissue paper. However, there are many times you might need to make a copy of a pattern:

- When using the patterns in this book! The patterns in all my books are printed on both sides of sturdy paper and are overlapped in some areas; they need to be traced so that you can still use the patterns on the other side.
- If you purchased a commercial tissue pattern and wish to retain all the sizes rather than just cutting out one size.
- When using vintage patterns, it's a good idea to preserve the original, since they are very delicate and tear easily.
- If you downloaded a PDF pattern and spent a lot of time taping the letter-size sheets together, you may want to trace only your size in case you want to make a different size in the future.

To trace a pattern like the ones included in this book, I like to use a corkboard as a surface and then put my clean pattern paper on top of the corkboard. Then I put the printed pattern on top and either use pattern weights or stick pins into the surface to hold all the layers in place. Run the spoked tracing wheel over the size line you wish to copy. Be sure to transfer any darts, notches, grainlines (the line with arrows on both ends that tells you how to place the pattern piece), circles, and other pattern markings. Then remove the printed pattern and take away the corkboard. On a hard table surface, go over the perforations made by the tracing wheel using a sharp pencil and your straight and curved rulers. Do not worry about adding seam allowances to the patterns in this book, as ⅝" (1.5 cm) is included on all pieces (except where noted otherwise).

Now that your pattern is traced and marked, you're ready to prep your fabric!

Getting Your Fabric On-Grain

Woven fabrics are made up of threads that run in different directions and make up the weave of the fabric (imagine how a basket is woven). These directions determine the fabric's grain: The crosswise grain is the threads that run perpendicular to the selvage; the lengthwise grain is parallel to the selvage; and the bias is at a 45-degree angle. Sometimes fabrics become off-grain, so that any garment made from them may hang awkwardly or twist around the body.

All you really need to know for now is that you need to get your fabric on-grain before cutting out your dress. This means that the lengthwise and crosswise threads are at 90-degree angles to each other, which ensures that the threads (and therefore your garment) hang correctly when worn. So what you need to do is get the cut edge of the fabric so that it is at a perfect 90-degree angle to the selvage and the cut edges align when the fabric is folded.

There are a couple of methods for making sure that the cut edge of fabric is on-grain. The first, and easiest, is ripping the fabric Hulk-style! Snip into the selvage of the fabric. See if you're able to rip the fabric by pulling the two sides of the snip apart. If the fabric rips easily, rip it all the way from selvage to selvage. The fabric will automatically rip on-grain (A).

If the fabric doesn't rip, you'll need to use a different method, and a good choice is pulling a thread. When you pull apart the two sides of the selvage snip, a couple of little threads will pop out. Grab one of those threads with your fingers or a pair of tweezers and pull until the fabric scrunches up and the thread breaks (B). When you pull out the thread, there will be an empty space in the weave of the fabric. Cut along this line until you get to the end of the empty space. Repeat the process of pulling a thread and cutting until you get to the opposite selvage.

Does the cut edge appear to be at a 90-degree angle to the selvage? You can check it with a gridded ruler. If it is not, pull on both cut edges of the fabric yardage on the bias until each edge is straight and perpendicular to the selvage. This straightens the grain throughout the fabric's length.

GETTING YOUR FABRIC ON-GRAIN

A. Ripping fabric on grainline

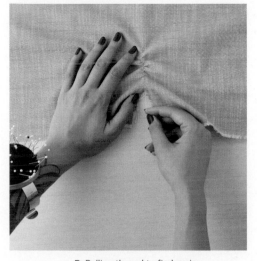

B. Pulling thread to find grain

Preparing Your Pattern Pieces

LAYING OUT YOUR FABRIC

Once your fabric is on-grain, you're ready to lay it out on a surface and pin the dress pattern pieces to it for cutting!

For most projects, you will be using a lengthwise cutting layout, meaning that the fabric is folded double with the fold along the lengthwise grain and the selvages aligned on top of each other (A). Sometimes, however, you may need to use a crosswise layout, where the fabric is folded double with the fold along its width and the straightened cut edges on top of each other. This gives you more room for cutting large skirt pieces (like for circle skirts) and also long rectangular pieces for skirts (like for the Patio Dress on page 126). Note that you also need to use the crosswise cutting layout when using a border print or fabric with an embroidered selvage (like for the Boatneck Dress on page 112).

When laying out fabric on the lengthwise grain, make sure that the selvages are precisely aligned on top of each other. Generally, you want the right sides of the fabric to be facing each other and the wrong side facing out. It's easier to transfer pattern markings to the fabric's wrong side this way.

PINNING THE PATTERN PIECES TO THE FABRIC

Once the fabric is laid out, you can begin to arrange pattern pieces on it. If a pattern piece is marked with a bracket and says "cut on fold," that means one piece is cut from the doubled fabric. Place the pattern's center-front or center-back edge so it is *directly* on the fold of the fabric. I often see students place the piece just shy of the fold, and this will affect the size of the piece and therefore your fit!

If a pattern piece doesn't have a "cut on fold" bracket, it will have what's called a floating

LAYING OUT YOUR FABRIC

A. Double layer of fabric; selvages on top of each other

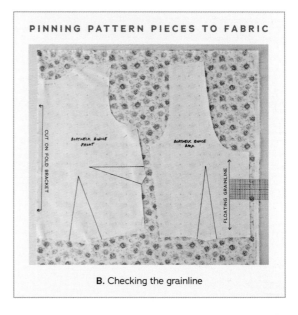

PINNING PATTERN PIECES TO FABRIC

B. Checking the grainline

grainline. This is a line with an arrow on either end, and it needs to be placed parallel to the selvage or the fabric's fold. This means the pattern is cut as two separate pieces with the fabric doubled. Lay the pattern on the fabric so that the grainline looks straight and parallel to the selvage, and then check it with a measuring tape or clear ruler (B). To do this, measure from one end of the floating grainline to the fold or selvage, making sure the ruler or tape is perpendicular to the fabric edge. Pin that end of the grainline in place and mentally record the measurement. At the other end of the floating grainline, measure the distance from the selvage or fold. If it does not match the first end's measurement, pivot the pattern piece until it is the same distance from the selvage or fold. Now pin around the rest of the pattern piece, placing pins around the outer edges of the pattern.

Finally, cut around your pattern pieces with fabric shears or a rotary cutter!

TRANSFERRING PATTERN MARKS AND NOTCHES

After your pattern pieces are cut, the next step is to transfer any markings like darts, circles, and pocket or button placement. I like to use wax- or chalk-coated dressmaker's tracing paper or a chalk pen for this purpose.

To transfer darts with dressmaker's tracing paper, first slip the tracing paper between the top layer of fabric and the pattern piece, with the colorful side down. Trace the dart with a spoked tracing wheel. Remove the tracing paper. Next, place the tracing paper, colorful side up, underneath the bottom layer of fabric. Trace the marked dart again to transfer the marking. Make sure that you've pressed firmly enough to transfer the marks to the bottom layer.

You can also transfer marks like circles or dart points with a piece of chalk (or a disappearing-ink pen). Place the point of a pin through the mark you wish to transfer, and then lift up the pattern without moving the pin. Use the chalk to make a mark at the pin point (E). You can use this method to transfer darts without dressmaker's tracing paper by connecting the point of the dart to the snips you make at the leg of each dart (see next step).

TRANSFERRING PATTERN MARKS AND NOTCHES

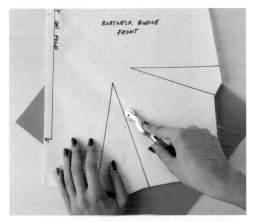

C. Using tracing paper and wheel to transfer dart

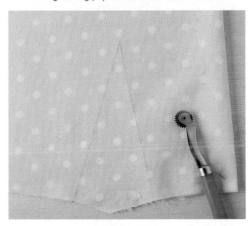

D. Traced dart

E. Using chalk to mark pin point

SNIPPING NOTCHES AND DART LEGS

A. Snip dart legs.

SNIPPING NOTCHES AND DART LEGS

Notches are pattern markings that help you match pieces along the seamlines as you sew. To transfer notches, make a tiny snip (through both the pattern and the fabric) into the point of the marked notch with the point of your scissors (A). Your snip should be ¼" (6 mm) long at maximum.

It's also a good idea to snip into the legs of the darts (the two lines that radiate from the dart point)—no more than ¼" (6 mm)—to help you match them up as you sew.

APPLYING INTERFACING

Fusible interfacing is a secondary material that is applied to parts of your dress for stability and firmness. For instance, neckline facings are always interfaced to help give shape and structure to the neckline and help the facing stay in place. Your pattern will tell you which pieces, if any, to cut out in fusible interfacing.

My favorite types of fusible interfacing for simple dressmaking projects are tricot (a sheer knit interfacing) and lightweight woven (a cotton-blend fabric interfacing), both with an adhesive coating on one side for fusing with heat. I always avoid nonwoven interfacing as it is very stiff and paper-like; it doesn't drape well in a garment.

You'll notice that fusible interfacing has a smooth side and a rough side. The rough side is the one coated with glue, which is the side that is fused to the fabric. Always make sure that you have the glue side down when you're ironing interfacing, or it will stick to your iron!

Lay the interfacing, glue side down, onto the wrong side of the fabric garment piece. Spritz with water from a spray bottle to dampen. Lay a sheer press cloth on top of the piece. Apply an iron on high heat, pressing down for ten to fifteen seconds before moving to the next spot (B). Do not slide the iron back and forth; instead pick it up and move it. Let the piece sit to cool and dry.

I also use 1¼"- (3.2 cm-) wide strips of interfacing to stabilize my zipper openings, and these strips are applied in the same way. You can either purchase precut rolls of interfacing (see Resources, page 138) or cut your own strips from fusible interfacing yardage.

APPLYING INTERFACING

B. Use a press cloth and apply interfacing with iron.

STAYSTITCHING

Staystitching is a preparatory step that prevents certain areas of a garment from stretching out as you're working. For instance, a neckline is often curved (meaning parts of it are on the bias), so it can stretch out if pulled during the dress construction. To counteract any stretching, use staystitching around necklines and any other curved edges that need to keep their shape.

Staystitching is simply a line of machine stitching done on a single layer, within the seam allowance, using a 2.5-mm stitch length. It must be done in a certain direction. On a neckline, stitch from the shoulder toward the center front; backstitch (sew in reverse for a couple of stitches) at center front. Then turn your work over and repeat the staystitching, again from shoulder to center front, on the other half of the neckline (C). As you sew, be careful not to pull, stretch, or distort the garment section. Staystitch in the same way on the back neckline: from shoulder to center back (D).

SERGE-FINISHING SEAM ALLOWANCES

This is the last step before putting your dress together! Using a serger as your seam finish method is totally optional, as I know investing in a serger isn't something everyone is ready to do when they start sewing (and you'll find more methods for seam finishing in the next chapter). But serge-finishing is the one method that you can do *before* sewing the dress, so it's important to include here.

For this step, simply serge any vertical edges of the pattern pieces, like side seams and skirt

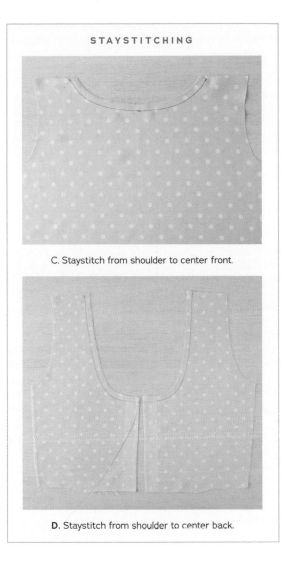

C. Staystitch from shoulder to center front.

D. Staystitch from shoulder to center back.

center-back edges: Run each piece through the serger, being careful not to actually trim away any fabric (you can even disengage your serger's blade to help you). Trim away the serger thread tails and you're ready to sew your dress!

CHAPTER FOUR

Dress Construction: The Basics

Now that you've done all the prep work from the last chapter, it's finally time to sew your dress. This is my favorite part. I love putting on some music and spending an afternoon with my sewing machine (and ironing board, of course—pressing is so important, ladies!). Once you're well acquainted with the construction order and process of sewing a dress, it becomes almost methodical and meditative to complete these steps. Enjoy the journey!

This chapter will give you the skills for sewing seams, darts, and other simple parts of dress construction. Chapter five will take you into the more complex steps, like sleeves and closures, as well as finishing details.

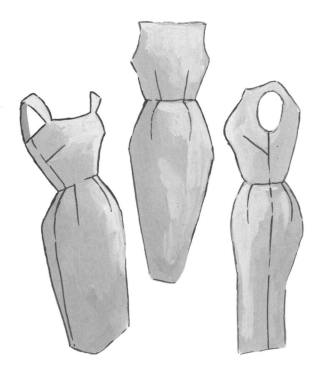

Dresses with darts

Darts

Darts are there to give a garment shape, which is crucial for that vintage look. Darts have "legs," the two lines that meet at the "point." These legs get sewn to each other, effectively removing the fabric in between them, shaping the dress and nipping it in a bit in all the right places. More importantly, darts create room for curvy parts of the body, like the bust and hips. Darts can sometimes look a little puckery when not sewn and pressed properly, so it's a good idea to spend some time working on your dart technique.

To sew a dart:

1. Bring the marked legs of the dart together (use the snips at the base of the dart as a guide) and place a pin vertically at the dart's point.

2. Place pins horizontally down the matched-up dart legs, making sure that the marked lines match perfectly on the top and bottom layers (A).

3. Place the piece in the machine, with the dart's wider end under the needle (the bulk of the dress will be to the left of the needle). Use a 2.5-mm stitch length. Backstitch at the beginning and then sew along the marked dart lines from the wide end to the point. When you get to the point of the dart, make the last two stitches so they're positioned on the fold of the fabric (this prevents puckers on the outside of the dart).

4. Do not backstitch at the point of the dart. Leave 3"- (7.6 cm-) long thread tails and tie them together in a double knot by hand, then trim the ends (B).

5. Press the dart from the wrong side of the fabric on a tailor's ham. Vertical darts should be pressed toward center front or center back. Horizontal darts should be pressed down (toward the hem of the dress). Take your time pressing. Position the bodice on the edge of the ham that mimics the curve of the body in the dart's location. Press the tip of the dart as flat as possible (C).

Sewing Seams

Here's how your dress comes together! When sewing seams, be careful to always position the fabric with the right sides together. The raw edges of the fabric should match exactly. Keep in mind that your pattern pieces won't always match perfectly at the top and bottom of a seam (for instance, at the front or back of a shoulder). This is because patterns are drafted to match at the seamlines, and then seam allowances are added, which means the shapes of the pieces you are matching may be slightly different. Just make sure that they match at the seamline ⅝" (1.5 cm) from the cut edge.

To sew a seam:

1. Position the two pieces of fabric right sides together, aligning the raw edges as closely as possible and matching the notches.

2. Place pins so that they are perpendicular to the raw edge of the fabric; this makes it easy to pull out the pins as you sew. A pin every 1" to 2" (2.5 cm to 5 cm) is fine in most cases.

3. Place the work in the machine and position the fabric so that the raw edge is aligned with the correct mark on the needle plate (usually the ⅝" [1.5 cm] mark). Lower the presser foot.

4. Sew for about three stitches, and then reverse the stitch back to the beginning using your machine's backstitch function.

5. Continue sewing to the end of the seam and then backstitch for three stitches again.

6. Press the seam allowances open (see page 40), unless the pattern instructions direct otherwise.

Note that when sewing a flared pattern piece (like the A-line skirt for the Swirl Dress on page 104), it's best to stitch from the bottom of the piece to the top. This is called directional stitching, and it helps avoid distorting the fabric's grain and stretching the piece out of shape.

PIVOTING A STITCHING LINE

To pivot while sewing a seam, stop with your needle down. Lift the presser foot and pivot the fabric to change direction, then lower the presser foot.

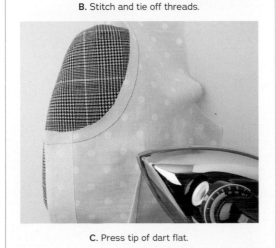

DARTS

A. Place pins along dart leg and at point.

B. Stitch and tie off threads.

C. Press tip of dart flat.

Pressing

Pressing is so important! Every time you sew something, you need to press it afterward. This is one of the things that will help your garment look more professional. You can sew a bunch of similar items (darts, seams, etc.) and then press them in a batch. The only rule is that you shouldn't sew an intersecting seam before the first one is pressed.

Keep your iron on the highest temperature safe for your fabric, and then press as you go. Use a press cloth if necessary on delicate fabrics. Most seam allowances should be pressed open (like butterfly wings) (A), but sometimes seam allowances are pressed as one unit in the same direction. In that case, press both seam allowances to one side as the pattern instructs.

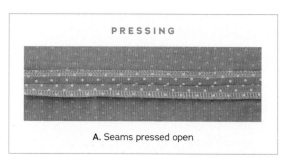

PRESSING

A. Seams pressed open

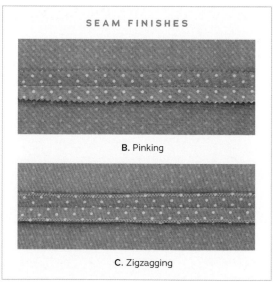

SEAM FINISHES

B. Pinking

C. Zigzagging

Seam Finishes

If you don't have a serger, you'll need to figure out another method for finishing your seams so that they don't fray as you wear and wash the garment. Here are a few options for finishing your seams.

PINKING (B): Pinking is a nice option—it's simple and quick, and it's also very vintage! Seamstresses have been finishing their seams this way for centuries, and it's a tried-and-true classic. Pinking shears create a zigzag edge on fabric, which looks like a row of tiny triangles. Because fabric does not fray on the bias, these little angled edges do not unravel. Pinking works best on crisp or tightly woven fabrics, like cotton shirting, rayon challis, or silk shantung. Test your pinking shears on a scrap of your fashion fabric first.

To pink seam allowances:

1. Sew the seam as usual.

2. Before pressing open, trim the seam allowance edges together using pinking shears.

3. Press the seam allowances open or to one side, depending on the pattern instructions.

ZIGZAGGING (C): This is another possible method, using your sewing machine stitches to create a barrier inside the raw edge to prevent it from unraveling beyond the stitches.

1. Sew the seam as usual and press the seam allowances open or to one side.

2. Set your machine for a zigzag stitch (2.5 mm long by 2.5 mm wide is fine).

3. If you've pressed the seam allowances open, zigzag each allowance separately, about 1/8" (3 mm) from the edge of the fabric. If you've pressed both allowances to one side, zigzag them together as a unit.

4. Trim the seam allowances just outside of the stitching.

OVERLOCK STITCHING: Finally, your sewing machine may have an overlock stitch that mimics a serger's overlocking stitch. This stitch can be an awesome alternative to pinking or zigzagging, so check your manual to see if it's a function included on your sewing machine. Use the included overlock foot and correct stitch along the edge of the fabric.

EDGESTITCHING AND TOPSTITCHING

After sewing a seam, the project instructions may call for you to secure it by edgestitching or topstitching. These stitches are also used on things like hems, pockets, and the opening for the wrap tie on the Swirl Dress (page 104).

EDGESTITCHING: To edgestitch, sew ¹⁄₁₆" to ⅛" (1.6 mm to 3 mm) from the fold or seam. I like to use an edgestitch foot, which has a blade that runs down the center of the foot. Align the blade with the fold or seamline and then move your needle to the side you are edgestitching. As you stitch, keep the blade aligned with the fold or seam; this will keep your stitching consistent and straight.

TOPSTITCHING: Topstitching is similar to edgestitching; it's just done at a wider distance, usually ¼" (6 mm) from a seam or fold. Most presser feet measure ¼" (6 mm) from the needle position to either the foot's outer edge or to a groove on the foot near the outer edge, so using this as a guide is a great technique for topstitching. Align the edge of your presser foot with the fold or seam and, with your needle in the center position, topstitch.

Keep in mind that topstitching can also be done in a contrasting-color thread for a decorative effect (though you'll want to be sure that your stitching is very straight), and you can also lengthen the stitches to call more attention to them.

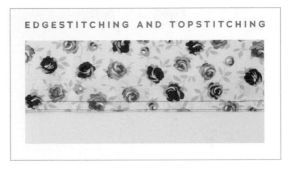

EDGESTITCHING AND TOPSTITCHING

GATHERING

D. Pull fabric along bobbin threads.

Gathering

Gathering is when fabric is pulled together to create fullness, and it's used all the time in vintage-style dresses: Think full and fluffy skirts, like the one on the Boatneck Dress on page 112, and the sweet neckline of the Swirl Dress on page 104.

To create gathers, set your machine for a 4-mm stitch length. In the area to be gathered, stitch using a ½" (1.3 cm) seam allowance. Leave thread tails that are at least a couple inches long. Stitch again next to the first row of stitching, this time using a ¼" (6 mm) seam allowance. Grab both bobbin threads on one end of the stitching and begin to pull the fabric along the threads, scrunching up the fabric as you go (D). Continue in this way, moving the fabric down the thread until the fabric is as gathered as you like. The gathered piece usually gets sewn to a flat piece, securing the gathers.

The Ruffler and Narrow Hemmer Feet

I love adding ruffles to dresses, and a tiered skirt like on the Patio Dress (page 126) is one of my favorite vintage styles. However, I have very little patience for gathering yards and yards of fabric by hand and then hemming it, which is where the ruffler and hemmer feet (shown on page 13) come in!

RUFFLER FOOT: The ruffler foot is an attachment that forms tiny pleats in your fabric that resemble gathers when sewn. The most important thing to understand about the ruffler foot is that it is not a substitute for machine gathering, as the pleats formed by the ruffler are not adjustable. You must ruffle a piece of fabric to the correct length so that it fits whatever seam it joins (or ruffle a longer piece and then cut it down to size). Because of this, I always test a 10" (25 cm) strip of fabric and see what length it reduces to after being ruffled. If it reduces to 5" (13 cm), I know I'll need approximately twice as much fabric as the area the ruffle will be sewn into.

When attaching the ruffler foot to your machine, make sure to follow the machine's instructions, as there's an "arm" that needs to be hooked onto your needle screw extension.

There are several settings on the ruffler foot; the lever in the front with numbers on it is the most important. If set to 1, that means the foot makes a pleat every stitch. If set to 6, the foot makes a pleat every six stitches, and so on. I always set mine to 1, as this best replicates the look of gathers.

There is also a screw near the front of the foot; this regulates how deep the pleats are.

Additionally, you can adjust how tight the pleats are (i.e., how much fabric is taken up when pleated) by adjusting the stitch length. Longer stitches mean a fuller, fluffier ruffle.

NARROW HEMMER FOOT: After ruffling, I usually hem the bottom of the ruffle before attaching it to a dress, as it's easier to work with when it's a smaller piece. The narrow hemmer foot is great for this, as it's specifically made to create a fine hem very quickly and it works especially well on straight edges. I'll warn you that it can take a little while to get the hang of, but it's awesome once you do.

Note how the narrow hemmer has a scroll-like feature on the front of the foot. This is where you feed the fabric through, and the scroll rolls the fabric to create the narrow hem. Situate your fabric under the presser foot with the raw edge curled around the scroll on the foot. As you sew, the edge should wrap around the scroll and then double over on itself. Start stitching, holding the curled fabric in front of the foot with your right thumb and index finger. Continue feeding the fabric in this way, stitching slowly and making sure the fabric stays correctly rolled around the scroll. The beginning and end of the hem are especially tricky, so it's a good idea to have a couple of extra inches to work with at both ends.

Once the fabric is ruffled and hemmed, switch back to the regular presser foot to stitch the ruffle to the bottom of a skirt (or anywhere else you like), with right sides together as usual.

Elastic Shirring

Elastic shirring is a method of creating stretch in a woven fabric by using elastic thread in the bobbin. I love this for creating a cinched waist on a voluminous dress like the Popover Dress on page 90. Elastic shirring was common on '50s bathing suits and sundresses, and I love incorporating it into my designs, both for its look and comfort.

You'll need elastic thread for this, which you can find either in the thread department or near the elastic in your local sewing shop.

To shirr with elastic thread:

1. It's usually recommended that you wind elastic thread onto a bobbin by hand. As you're winding, you'll need to stretch the thread a little so there's a bit of tension. I just give mine a little tug when starting to wind. Alternatively, I've found that it is actually possible to wind elastic thread onto a bobbin by machine. You just need to go slowly, and instead of snapping the elastic thread into the machine's tension disc (the silver circle you usually secure your thread into), you will need to hook it underneath your finger. I recommend winding a couple of bobbins to start, since the elastic thread is fairly thick and not much fits on one bobbin.

2. Load the bobbin into the machine, pull up the elastic thread, and treat it as regular bobbin thread. Depending on your machine, you may need to loosen the bobbin tension so the elastic feeds through easily without stretching too much. Stitch as normal from here on, backstitching at the beginning. All stitching is done from the right side of the fabric so that the elastic is on

ELASTIC SHIRRING

the wrong side of the dress. You can lengthen the stitch to create more stretchiness. You may also need to tighten the needle thread tension. Do a practice run to see what works for your machine.

3. As you sew, check the bobbin regularly so you know when it is nearly empty. When you reach the end of a bobbin thread, either backstitch or tie the threads off by hand on the wrong side of the dress.

4. After completing the shirring, use an iron to apply steam to the elastic thread on the wrong side. It will shrink up before your very eyes!

Note that some computerized machines do not handle elastic thread in the bobbin. Test your machine first before committing to a project with shirring.

CHAPTER FIVE

Dress Construction: Essential Skills

This chapter is devoted to the more complex steps of dressmaking. These include edge finishes, such as facings and bias bindings, as well as hand stitches and hem finishes. You'll also learn steps for more intermediate dressmaking, like setting in sleeves, and closures like lapped zippers and buttonholes. None of these are especially difficult skills to execute; they just take a little patience and practice. Once you master these skills, you will be able to sew almost any dress that comes your way!

A. Stitch facing to garment.

B. Grade seam allowances.

C. Clip and/or notch seam allowances.

D. Understitch the facing.

Facings

Facings are a type of edge finish for a garment, applied most often to necklines and armholes, but also to pockets, front shirt or jacket edges, and hemlines. A facing is a separate piece that matches the shape of the garment's edge. It is almost always reinforced with fusible interfacing to stiffen it and help keep its shape. It is then sewn to the garment right sides together and turned to the inside. Pay special attention to the steps that come after stitching (grading, notching, and clipping), as these are the techniques that help your dress look professionally finished.

To apply a facing:

1. Apply fusible interfacing, like a knit tricot or lightweight woven fusible interfacing, to the facing pieces. Stitch any necessary seams, like the shoulder seams on a neckline facing unit. Press seam allowances open.

2. Pin the facing to the garment right sides together, matching the raw edges. Stitch together with a ⅝" (1.5 cm) seam allowance (A).

3. *Grade* the facing seam allowances to reduce bulk: Trim the facing seam allowance down to a scant ¼" (6 mm) wide and the garment seam allowance to ⅜" (1 cm) wide (B). (Having the seam allowances two different widths means they won't sit right on top of each other and create an ugly ridge visible from the outside of your finished garment.)

4. *Clip and/or notch* the seam allowances: This step is crucial in achieving a neckline that doesn't bunch and lays nice and smooth. On any inner (concave) curves, clip straight into the seam allowances about every ½" (1.3 cm), being careful not to cut the stitches. On any outer (convex) curves, notch the seam allowances by cutting out small triangles. Remember, inner curves always mean clipping (straight snips) and outer curves always mean notches (cut-out triangles) (C).

5. *Understitch* the facing: Flip the facing away from the garment and position the seam allowances underneath the facing. Stitch about ¹⁄₁₆" to ⅛" (1.6 mm to 3 mm) to the right of the seamline, sewing through the seam allowances beneath the facing (D).

6. Turn the facing back to the wrong side of the garment. Press the facing, rolling the understitching to the wrong side to produce a nice crisp edge.

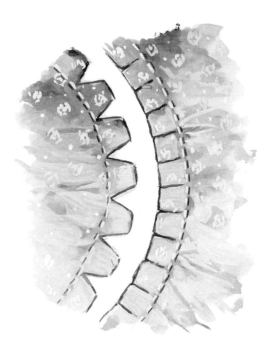

Notching vs. clipping

SECURING FACINGS

Facings create a nicely finished edge, but they can easily pop out of a neckline or armhole if they're not secured properly on the inside of the dress. There are two ways to secure a facing:

- **HAND-STITCHING:** Hand-stitch it in place to the seam allowances below it, such as at a center-front seam or shoulder seams. Use several hand stitches on top of each other to tack the facing in place, stitching only to the seam allowance underneath (not the outside of the dress).

SECURING FACINGS

E. Stitching in the ditch

- **STITCHING IN THE DITCH:** This is a fast and easy machine method that can be used to secure a facing to any seam, such as a neckline facing to a shoulder seam, center-back, or center-front seam. From the right side of the garment, pin the facing underneath to the seam, aligning the facing and garment seamlines. With the needle perfectly aligned in the center of the seamline (the "ditch"), sew a line of straight stitches while holding the garment taut. If positioned properly, the stitching will disappear within the seamline and be undetectable (E).

Bias Edge Finishes

A bias facing is a nice low-bulk way to finish a neckline or armhole. It's much narrower than a shaped facing, so it's a great solution for a sleeveless dress that has a neckline facing but needs a finish for the armholes (like the Boatneck Dress on page 112). You can buy ready-cut bias tape for this purpose (it's also handy for enclosing the raw edges of a garment for a contrast look), but it's very easy to just cut your

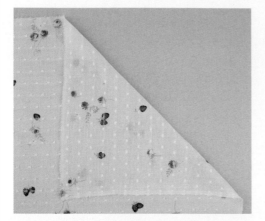

A. Fold fabric at a 45-degree angle.

B. Cut bias strips with ruler and rotary cutter.

can now cut strips of the fabric to the desired width using the rotary cutter and ruler (A, B).

A good width for a bias facing strip is the seam allowance width plus twice the desired finished width of the bias facing. I like to use 1½"- (3.8 cm-) wide strips, which accounts for a ⅝" (1.5 cm) seam allowance, a finished ⅜" (1 cm) bias facing, plus a little extra for "turn of cloth" (the fabric that gets taken up by a fold). The strip should be long enough to go around the opening you are finishing, plus a seam allowance at each end.

Sewing a Bias Facing

Here are the steps to a nicely finished bias facing. They are demonstrated on an armhole facing, but this can also be used around a neckline or even a hemline.

1. Form the bias strip into a ring by stitching the short ends of the strip right sides together. Press the seam allowances open.

2. Pin the ring to the armhole (or other opening), matching the strip's seam to the side seam on the dress (C).

3. Stitch around the armhole, using your usual seam allowance. Grade and clip or notch into the seam allowances, and understitch the bias facing following the instructions for a facing on page 47 (D).

4. Turn the seam allowances and bias facing to the wrong side of the armhole, and then fold under the raw edge of the facing so that it is now doubled. Press and pin in place.

5. Secure the facing by hand-stitching with a slipstitch (see page 57). Alternatively, you can edgestitch the fold in place from the wrong side of the garment, but keep in mind that this will result in visible stitching on the right side of the dress (E).

own bias strips from the garment fabric. Fabric cut on the bias (45-degree angle) stretches and curves easily, so bias strips are great for finishing edges of all shapes.

To cut bias strips, fold up a corner of the fabric so that the corner and the cut edge meet the fabric selvage and the fold forms a 45-degree angle. (You can make sure of the angle by using a clear ruler to check that the selvages are perpendicular to each other.) This fold forms the "true bias" of the fabric. Crease the fabric's fold, then unfold the fabric. Cut along the crease; a rotary cutter and clear ruler are fantastic tools for this purpose. From the edge that you just cut, you

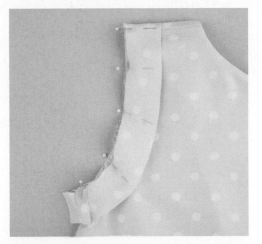

SEWING A BIAS FACING

A. Pin bias ring to garment.

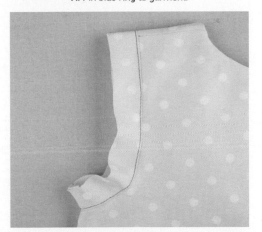

B. Understitch bias facing.

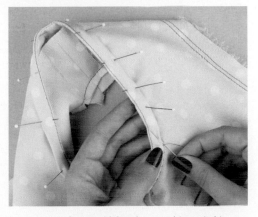

C. Secure facing with hand- or machine-stitching.

Sleeves

Many new seamstresses fear sleeves, but there's nothing to be concerned about! Once you understand how sleeves work and give them some practice, you'll see that setting in a sleeve can be (dare I say it) fun and exciting.

A set-in sleeve has a "cap," an outwardly rounded (convex) part that goes around your shoulder where it meets your torso. However, the armhole of a dress is rounded in an inner (concave) curve. These two opposing curves must be sewn together to fit the contours of your body. To further complicate matters, the sleeve cap is usually slightly longer than the armhole and must be "eased in" to create the necessary shape and allow for your body's movements. (Spend some time looking at someone's arm and shoulder where it meets their torso and it will start to make sense, I swear!)

◄ CAP

Take a moment to look at a sleeve pattern. You can tell the front of the sleeve from the back by the number of notches: The front of the sleeve has a single notch, while the back of the sleeve has two notches. There is a single notch at the top of the sleeve cap (on some patterns, this is marked with a small circle), where it must meet the shoulder seam of the bodice. It's very important to use these notches correctly, or your sleeve will hang strangely because sleeves are asymmetrical from front to back. The sleeve cap gets slightly gathered, or eased, between the front and back notches and set into the dress's armhole.

EASING THE SLEEVE CAP

The first step in sewing a set-in sleeve is to ease the cap, or pull it up slightly so that it will fit into the dress's armhole. This method uses two rows of gathering stitches; there are other methods out there (check out my book *Gertie's Ultimate Dress Book* if you are interested in learning other techniques), but this is the classic way, and the method you should learn first.

1. Using a long stitch (4 mm to 5 mm), stitch the sleeve cap between the notches, using a ½" (1.3 cm) seam allowance. Repeat with a ¼" (6 mm) seam allowance (A).

2. Pull up the bobbin threads to slightly gather the sleeve cap. Distribute the gathers evenly to avoid having any visible gathers or tucks on the seamline itself. The raw edge of the sleeve cap will form ruffles.

SETTING THE SLEEVE INTO THE DRESS

Now that your sleeve cap is eased, it's time to sew the sleeve to the bodice.

1. Sew the underarm seam on the sleeve, with right sides together. Press the seam allowances open.

2. Pin the sleeve to the armhole, right sides together. Start at the shoulder seam, matching

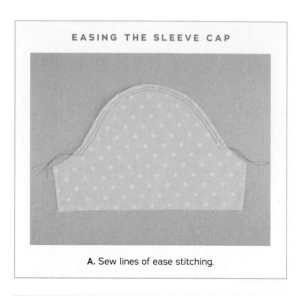

EASING THE SLEEVE CAP

A. Sew lines of ease stitching.

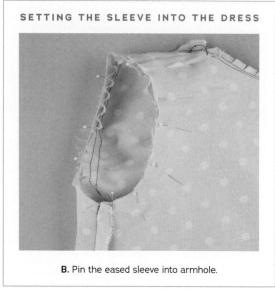

SETTING THE SLEEVE INTO THE DRESS

B. Pin the eased sleeve into armhole.

it to the notch at the top of the sleeve cap. Place the pins on the armhole side. Now move to the underarm, matching the underarm seams to the side seams of the bodice. Next, match the front and back sleeve cap notches to the notches on the armhole. Finally, pin the eased portion of the sleeve cap. (Note that the raw edge of the sleeve cap seam allowance is ruffled, while the raw edge of the armhole seam allowance is not. This is what you want!)

If the sleeve is still too big for the armhole, pull the gathering stitches slightly to gently gather a bit more of the sleeve's ease (B).

3. Once the sleeve is pinned into the armhole, machine-sew the seam. If you're worried about puckers, you may wish to machine- or hand-baste the sleeve first (sew temporarily with a long stitch). Start and end the stitching at the underarm.

4. Check the outside of the sleeve for puckers or unintentional pleats. If you see any, unpick the stitching in that section of the sleeve. Smooth out the pucker and restitch.

5. Reinforce the underarm between the sleeve cap notches by stitching again ⅛" (3 mm) outside the seam. Trim the seam allowances close to the second line of stitching, but leave the entire seam allowance intact on the upper portion of the sleeve—press those seam allowances toward the sleeve and finish them as one.

Lapped Zippers

There are several types of zipper applications you may choose from, but a lapped zipper is my favorite. It has a charmingly old-fashioned look (this is the style that was popular in the '50s, my favorite fashion era), and it's very strong, which is a great choice for closely fitted bodices.

1. On the garment's wrong side, stabilize the seam allowances of the zipper opening with 1¼"- (3.2 cm-) wide strips of fusible interfacing (you can also use precut fusible stay tape to save time; see Resources, page 138). This stabilizer will keep the seam allowances from stretching out vertically as you sew the zipper in place; stretching can cause unpleasant things like buckling and mismatched seams.

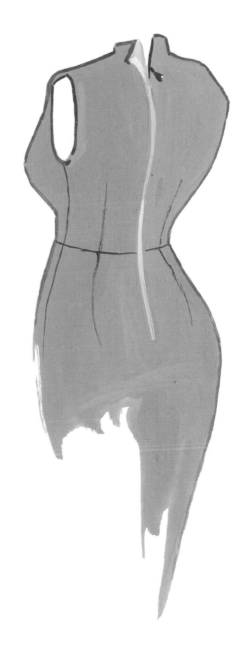

2. As you look at the back of the dress, the right side of the opening is the underlap side and the left side is the overlap side. On the underlap side, press the seam allowance to the wrong side by ½" (1.3 cm). Use a ruler and measure carefully. On the overlap side, press the seam allowance to the wrong side by the usual ⅝" (1.5 cm).

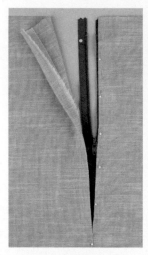

A. Pin zipper to underlap.

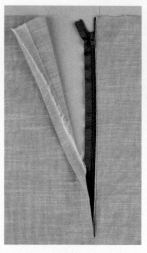

B. Stitch zipper to underlap.

C. Pin overlap side of zipper.

D. Topstitch overlap.

3. Working on a flat surface, place the zipper underneath the underlap seam allowance so that the fold you pressed is right next to the zipper teeth. The top zipper stop should be ⅝" (1.5 cm) below the raw edge of the neckline. Pin the zipper in place (A).

4. Open the zipper halfway. Using a zipper foot, stitch close to the zipper teeth, from the top to the bottom. When you get close to the zipper pull, stop stitching with the needle down, raise the presser foot, and close the zipper to get the pull out of the way. Lower the presser foot again and finish stitching the zipper in place (B).

5. Return to your flat surface. Place the overlap side of the zipper opening over the zipper, so that it just covers the line of stitching you made in step 4. Pin through all the layers to the left of the zipper teeth (C). Make sure that any horizontal seamlines (like midriff seams or waistline seams) match on either side of the zipper. (I start by matching at the waistline first, then I pin down to the base of the zipper. Next, I return to the neckline and match there, and then pin down to the waistline. This specific order is very helpful in getting both sides of your zipper opening to match each other.)

6. Open the zipper all the way. Using a zipper foot (depending on the type of foot, you may need to adjust your needle so that it is on the other side of the foot), topstitch ⅜" (1 cm) to the left of the overlap fold. When you get as close to the bottom as you can without stitching over the pull, stop stitching with the needle down, raise the presser foot, and close the zipper to get the pull out of the way. Lower the presser foot again and continue topstitching. At the base of the zipper opening, pivot the garment and stitch horizontally along the bottom, forming an L shape. (You can mark in your topstitching line at the bottom of the zipper first if you like.) Backstitch for a couple of stitches at the end (D).

Inside view of the Patio Dress with Short Sleeves (p. 133)

Buttons and Buttonholes

Buttons come in so many lovely varieties, colors, shapes, and sizes that it's unusual for a sewing enthusiast not to have a stash of beloved buttons saved up for a rainy day. I especially love shopping for buttons in vintage and antiques stores, where you can find the treasured button stashes of the seamstresses who came before us. What better way to honor them than by putting their buttons to good use on a new dress?

Buttons can be added to a dress in a purely decorative way, like on the pockets of the plaid Swirl Dress on page 111 or the sleeve accents on the Boatneck Dress sheath variation on page 119, or they can be functional, like on the waist sash on the square-neckline Chemise Dress on page 101. In the latter case, you will need to make buttonholes to correspond to the buttons.

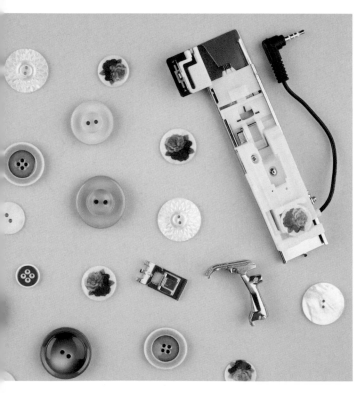

Buttonholes and buttonhole feet

MAKING BUTTONHOLES

Mechanical sewing machines generally make a multistep buttonhole, which requires you to turn a knob between buttonhole steps (which include the sides of the buttonhole and the bar tacks on each end). My beloved mechanical machine, for instance, makes a buttonhole in six steps, and I have to set it to each new step in the process when it's time. On the other end of the spectrum, my fancy computerized machine makes an automatic one-step buttonhole (in a variety of shapes, including a keyhole) and measures the size of the button to make a series of perfectly identical buttonholes. Most people prefer the ease of a one-step buttonhole, but either one works well.

Whichever type your machine does, make sure that you have the correct buttonhole presser foot. You can see the two presser feet for both of my machines in the image at left. The mechanical machine's foot is very simple and just has grooves in the bottom for the ridges on either side of the buttonhole to run smoothly under the foot. The foot for the computerized machine is large and complex-looking. It has a space where you insert the button so it can measure the button's size, and then it plugs into the machine directly to program the buttonhole.

The best advice I can give is to study your machine's manual thoroughly to understand exactly how your model works. While most finished buttonholes look similar to one another, the process to make them can vary greatly from machine to machine. And always make at least one buttonhole test before sewing a buttonhole onto your garment. Buttonhole mistakes are very difficult to remove, as the stitching is very dense. When testing, use the same number of fabric layers (including interfacing) that your garment will have (A).

When using a multistep buttonhole, you must mark in the length of the buttonhole

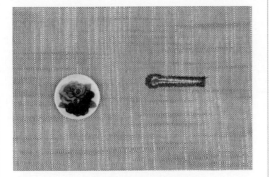

MAKING BUTTONHOLES

A. Always test buttonholes.

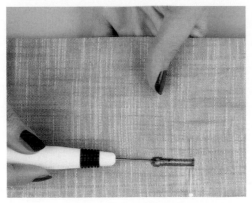

B. Place a pin before cutting.

yourself. Position the button on the garment and mark on either end (to the top and bottom for vertical buttonholes and to the right and left for horizontal buttonholes), adding ⅛" (3 mm) for room to pass the button through. Connect the two outer marks with a center line. Stitch the buttonhole following your marks.

To cut a buttonhole open, always put a pin at one end of the buttonhole to prevent accidentally cutting through stitches (the horror!). Use a seam ripper to then cut between the two sides of the buttonhole, away from yourself and toward the pin, stopping at the pin (B). Trim away any loose threads with small scissors.

To stitch on the corresponding button, always use doubled-up thread to hand-sew the button in

place, stitching through the button's holes to secure it. A shank-style button attaches by sewing through the hole in the shank on its back.

Hems

The hem is usually the last thing you sew when making a dress. For some styles, like the A-line skirt of the Swirl Dress (page 104), you will need to hang your dress for about twenty-four hours before hemming. This is because some fabrics can stretch out when cut on the bias, especially on a skirt. The center front of a flared skirt is on the straight grain, but its side seams are cut on a diagonal (the bias), the most stretchy direction of a fabric's grain. After letting the dress hang, inspect the hemline to see if it has stretched out of shape around the sides. If it looks longer in places, measure the hem and trim it.

To do this, it's best to have a friend to help or a dress form that you can hang the dress on. Measure up from the ground using a yardstick, marking the desired hem length with pins or chalk; this ensures the hemline is parallel to the floor. Take the dress off the form and connect the pins or marks to make a continuous line for the hem. Trim the hem allowance so that it is even all the way around; how deep you want the hem allowance depends on the style of skirt and the hemming method.

If you don't have a dress form or someone to help you, there are a few options. You can pin up the hem so that it looks even, try it on, and adjust in the mirror if necessary. Or you can measure down from the waistline so that the skirt is the same length all the way around, but note that this method may not work well if you have a fuller backside or hips, which can make a skirt shorter on the sides or in back.

For a straight hemline (like on any of the gathered skirts that are just rectangles), there won't be any stretching, so you can sew the hem without letting it hang or measuring and marking.

NARROW HEMS

A narrow hem is fantastic for flared skirts, like on the Swirl Dress (page 104), and for full, gathered, tiered skirts, like on the Patio Dress (page 126). It works best on light- to medium-weight fabrics. Leave a ½" (1.3 cm) hem allowance if you choose to use this method.

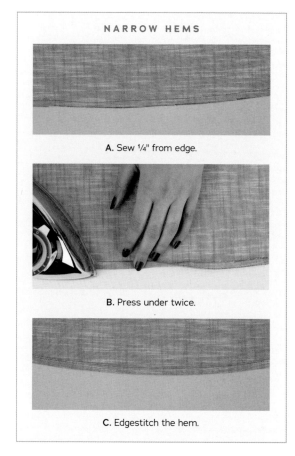

NARROW HEMS

A. Sew ¼" from edge.

B. Press under twice.

C. Edgestitch the hem.

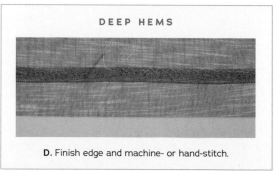

DEEP HEMS

D. Finish edge and machine- or hand-stitch.

1. Sew a row of machine stitching ¼" (6 mm) from the raw edge of the skirt hem (A).

2. Press under the hem allowance by ¼" (6 mm) all the way around, using the stitching as a guide. The stitching should just roll to the wrong side of the skirt (B).

3. Turn under the hem and press a second time, so you have a doubled ¼"- (6 mm-) deep hem. Pin in place if necessary.

4. Edgestitch the fold on the wrong side to secure the hem. I like to use my edgestitch foot for this (C).

DEEP HEMS

For straight skirts (like the Chemise Dress on page 94, or the Boatneck Dress sheath variation on page 119) a deeper hem can be nice, as it gives the skirt a little weight. It also works well for thicker fabrics. To use this type of hem, leave anywhere from 1¼" to 2" (3.2 cm to 5 cm) for a hem allowance.

1. Finish the raw edge of the hem by serging, stitching on hem lace (a prepacked lace specifically for hemming), or turning under ¼" (6 mm) and pressing.

2. Use a ruler to turn under the hem allowance evenly and press all the way around.

3. Secure the hem by edgestitching the fold or hand-stitching in place (D).

Hand-Stitching

The dresses in this book require minimal hand-finishing, but there are a couple of stitches that will come in handy for hemming when topstitching doesn't work well on a particular fabric, such as very textured fabrics or when you don't want to disrupt a print. Hand-stitching is also a lovely choice because you can make your stitches invisible by taking up just a thread or two of the outer fabric with each stitch. You'll also use hand stitches for securing facings on the inside of the dress.

SLIPSTITCHING

This stitch comes in handy when you are stitching a fold to a flat layer (for instance, a bias facing on an armhole).

Thread a hand-sewing needle and knot the end of the thread. First, anchor the thread by pulling it up through the folded edge of the hem. Working right to left, take a tiny stitch in the garment fabric (just pick up a thread or two with the needle) about ⅛" (3 mm) to the left of the anchored thread; pull the thread through. Insert the needle back into the fold of the hem about ¼" (6 mm) to the left and slide the needle inside the fold for about ¼" (6 mm), then bring it back out. Take a tiny stitch in the garment about ⅛" (3 mm) to the left above the fold. Continue alternating stitches inside the fold and in the garment fabric, positioning the stitches so they are between the two layers.

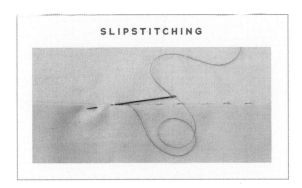

SLIPSTITCHING

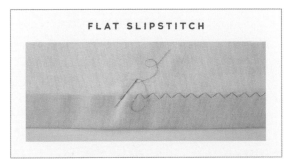

FLAT SLIPSTITCH

HAND-STITCHING BASICS

- Use a short single length of thread to prevent tangling. Measure out the thread so that it is the distance from your elbow to the tips of your fingers.
- Thread the needle and let about 2" (5 cm) of thread tail hang from the eye of the needle. Hold the needle at the base to secure the thread so it doesn't come unthreaded.
- Tie the thread in a secure knot. There are lots of fun tips for knotting thread; ask an experienced seamstress how she does it!
- When you're finished stitching or you need to rethread the needle, take several small stitches on top of each other rather than knotting off. This gives a nice flat finish.

FLAT SLIPSTITCH

I like this method for deep hems and anywhere one flat layer is secured to another. Stitches will be visible on the wrong side of the garment, but not on the right side—if you take a small enough stitch. Again, the idea is that you just need to pick up a thread or two of the outer fabric when stitching; this prevents any bumps or puckers on the right side of the fabric.

Anchor the thread by pulling it up through the bottom layer of fabric and take a tiny horizontal stitch in the top layer of fabric about ¼" (6 mm) to the left of the anchoring stitch. Then, without pulling the needle through yet, take a similar stitch in the bottom layer, also ¼" (6 mm) to the left. Pull the thread through. Continue in this manner, holding the needle on a diagonal, and taking up a stitch from each layer before pulling the needle through the fabric.

CHAPTER SIX

Trims and Flourishes

Sometimes a beautiful trim can turn the most basic dress into something sublime. The easy dresses in this book are wonderful canvases for playing around with trim ideas like rows of rickrack, accent bows, or hemline fringe. One of my favorite ways to find inspiration for trim ideas is to look at vintage dresses online or in person. For instance, the idea for the double bias pockets with button accents on the plaid Swirl Dress (page 111) was borrowed from a '50s dress I own and adore.

Flat Trim

Flat trim includes fringe, rickrack, ribbons, lace, and anything that can be applied directly to a garment and topstitched in place. Keep in mind that some trims are not appropriate around curves because they can't be shaped (like ribbon, for instance), so always pin trim onto your garment to test it first.

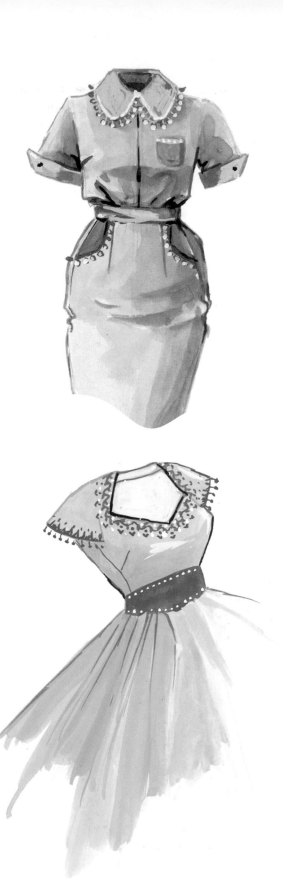

Assorted trims

To sew a trim like rickrack, pin it in place on your dress. You can mark a chalk line first if that helps you place it evenly around a neckline or hem. Stitch in place directly down the center of the trim. An edgestitch foot (with the needle set to the center position) can be helpful for keeping your stitches even.

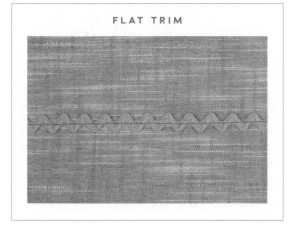

FLAT TRIM

For some trims, like fringe and pompoms, you may need to stitch at one edge of the trim rather than down the center. These trims are attached to tapes so they can be secured to a garment.

Besides stitching trims onto a garment's surface, you can explore other options:

- Sandwich some rickrack within a pocket's top edge so just the scalloped edge peeks out.
- Place some fringe or large pompoms behind a hem for some swishy fun.
- Insert dangling trim (like fringe or pompoms) into the tiers on a ruffled skirt, like the Patio Dress (page 126). Along the bottom edge of a tier, machine-baste the trim so that its tape is situated within the seam allowance and the fringe or pompoms are on its right side, facing away from the seam allowance. After gathering the next tier, pin and stitch it right sides together to the previous tier, with the trim sandwiched between the two layers.

Trim on Chemise Dress, Fringe Cocktail Variation (page 103)

Pockets

Pockets put the "fun" back in functional! I don't know a single woman who doesn't love a dress with pockets; they're great for carrying your phone, lipstick, candy, and all your other treasures—while simultaneously looking cute! Patch pockets can be applied to the outside of any skirt. You can use the flap pocket pattern in the book or make your own!

1. Fold the pocket's upper hem (at least 1" [2.5 cm]) to the right side along the marked hemline and press and pin in place.

2. Stitch just within the seam allowance around the two vertical sides and lower edge of the pocket, catching the folded hem allowance from step 1; this stitching becomes a pressing guide in the next steps (A).

POCKETS

A. Stitch around three sides.

B. Press in edges.

C. Edgestitch to dress.

D. Sew bar tack.

POCKET DESIGN
IDEAS

**POCKET DESIGN
IDEAS**

- Cut a plaid or striped fabric on the bias for a striking effect.
- Use a contrasting color fabric or even use a second print as an accent to the garment's print.
- Try changing the shape of the pocket, like curving the bottom edge.
- Stitch a flat trim like lace, pompoms, or rickrack across the upper edge of the pocket.
- Layer pockets asymmetrically on top of each other as on the plaid Swirl Dress (below).

3. Trim the upper corners of the pockets and turn the hem allowance to the wrong side. Use the guide stitching to turn under and press the seam allowances around the pocket's sides and lower edge (B).

4. Position the pocket on the garment (make sure it is straight and even with its opposing pocket, if applicable) and pin and baste in place.

5. Secure with edgestitching by machine (C).

6. If desired, you can add another layer of security to your pockets by sewing bar tacks in the upper corners. Set your machine to a narrow zigzag stitch (about 1 mm wide) with a very short stitch length (around 0.5 mm) and stitch over where the upper edge of the pocket attaches to the garment for about ¼" (6 mm). This is where a pocket gets the most stress, and the bar tack reinforces the area (D).

Bows

Always feminine and flirty, bows are a great addition to any vintage-inspired dress. Stitch a fabric bow at a neckline or on a sleeve hem, like I did for the Boatneck Dress sheath variation on page 119. Making a bow is just a process of sewing rectangles!

1. Figure out your desired dimensions for the bow. Cut a fabric rectangle that is twice the desired width (plus seam allowances) by the desired length (plus seam allowances). I like to use ¼" (6 mm) seam allowances on bows, as it means less trimming.

2. Fold the fabric lengthwise, right sides together, and sew around the cut edges, leaving an opening for turning. Clip the corners and turn the piece right side out (A).

3. Press. Sew the opening closed by hand using a slipstitch.

4. Pinch the rectangle at the center so it looks like a piece of bowtie pasta. Secure with a hand stitch through the entire width. At this point, you can cover the center of the bow with a button and stitch directly to your dress. Alternatively, you can make a second rectangle to cover the center and mimic a knot.

5. To add a knot, figure out the dimensions for the knot rectangle. It needs to be long enough to wrap around the center of the bow (plus seam allowances), and it should be double the desired finished width (plus seam allowances).

6. Fold the fabric rectangle lengthwise, right sides together, and stitch the long edge. Turn the tube right side out through one open end and press flat.

7. Wrap the knot rectangle around the bow, with the raw edges overlapped in the back (turn

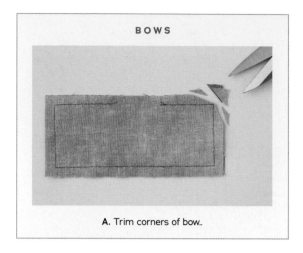

BOWS

A. Trim corners of bow..

under the raw edge of the end on top for a clean finish). Hand-sew the short ends together to secure the knot.

8. Sew the bow to your dress by tacking it from behind with hand stitches.

Bias Tubing

Bias tubing is simply bias strips of fabric sewn into tubes and then turned right side out. Though the concept is simple, there are many lovely applications for this type of trim. I love bias tubing for bows, spaghetti straps, and other swirls and accents on a dress.

1. Cut strips of fabric on the true bias. (Find the true bias by folding a corner of the fabric back on itself to get a 45-degree angle on the fold as described on page 48; this fold is the bias.) Cut strips with a clear ruler and rotary cutter, about 1¼" (3.2 cm) wide.

2. With right sides together, fold a strip in half along the length.

3. Sew the strip with the folded edge to the right of your needle using a ⅛" (3 mm) seam

BIAS TUBING

A. Sew with fold to right of needle.

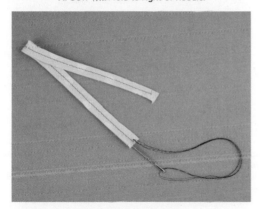

B. Turn tube right side out.

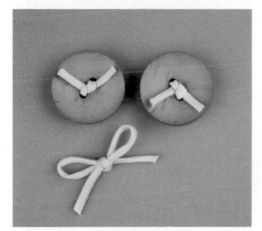

C. Tie into bows, knots, or other trim.

allowance (A). (Sewing with the fold on the right makes the finished width of the tubing more consistent and accurate.)

4. Trim the tube seam allowances down to a scant ⅛" (3 mm).

5. Thread a large needle (a dull tapestry needle, preferably) with two strands of thread, double them, and tie a strong knot at the end (this means you will have four strands of thread). Take a stitch through the seam allowances on one end of the tube. Thread the needle through the tube, eye end (the dull side) first if using a sharp needle. Pull the needle through the tube, gently working the end of the tube until it turns into itself (this takes a little patience). Pull the entire tube right side out (B). (There is an amazing tool called a Fasturn set that makes much quicker work of this, but it is on the pricey side. It's definitely worth looking into if you find yourself turning lots of tubes!)

6. Apply the tubing to your dress as desired. You can use the tubes as spaghetti straps or skinny bows, or pin them in swirly designs onto your dress and then hand-stitch them in place from the wrong side of the dress. I love how bias tubing looks threaded through oversize buttons with large holes, as a decorative accent on a dress. If the raw ends of the tube are left exposed, cut them neatly or tie them into little knots and trim the ends (they won't fray, since they're on the bias). Alternatively, you may tuck the raw ends into the tube and hand-stitch the tubes closed at the ends (C).

CHAPTER SEVEN

Fitting

Fitting can be an especially challenging part of sewing. After all, we spend so much time working on our construction skills, and we want the finished garments to look stunning! It's very rare that someone will fit exactly into a pattern's size chart; in fact, it's rarer for someone to conform to it exactly. So please don't be put off by thinking that your body is weird or that a particular pattern is difficult to fit. Fitting adjustments are just part of sewing (and it makes it so rewarding when you achieve a perfectly fitting frock!). This is an area where it can be really helpful to get advice from a fellow sewing enthusiast with fitting experience. Take a class, ask your grandma, or even join a Facebook sewing group, where you can post photos and get fitting help from others. You can do it!

Fitting Strategies

The first thing you want to do is look at the size chart for the pattern you are making. (It's on page 83 for the patterns in this book.) Above all else, do not simply choose a size based on what you would buy in a store! Pattern sizing can be totally different from ready-to-wear sizing; some of the major pattern companies haven't changed their size charts in decades, meaning that you may actually be a couple of sizes larger in a pattern than you anticipated. Don't worry about the size numbers; just focus on the measurements. Remember the favorite adage of sewists everywhere: When you make it yourself, it's whatever size you say it is!

After choosing a size, decide if there are any preliminary adjustments you need to make. For instance, if you're tall, you may always need to add length to a bodice. As you sew more, you'll get to know your body and what changes

you require. Once you've made those usual adjustments, it's a good idea to make a muslin test version (see page 73) so that you can see, in fabric on your body, how the garment will fit. The muslin will most likely give you information on other areas you want to tweak (this is where I usually find myself taking little tucks and pinches out, or deciding I need more room somewhere). Finally, go back to the paper pattern and transfer these changes to it. If you had a lot of changes, you may wish to make a new muslin at this point. Once you feel confident with your pattern, you can (finally!) cut it out in your fabric.

If you find the process daunting, it's a good idea to start with projects that aren't designed to require a super-precise fit. For instance, the Popover Dress in this book (page 84) has a full silhouette that will work on a lot of body types with a minimum of fitting fuss.

Finished Measurements

In addition to the size chart, the most useful pieces of information are the finished garment measurements. These measurements tell you the dimensions of a garment after it has been sewn. For a garment made from woven fabric, these measurements are larger than your body measurements, because you usually don't want a garment to fit like a second skin—you want to have ease to move and breathe and eat. I've started including finished measurements for all my patterns because I find it to be so helpful in choosing a size. Everyone has different standards for how they like their clothing to fit (I tend to like mine on the snugger side, while many people can't stand the feel of a garment that fits closely to the body). I can compare the finished garment measurements with a similar garment I already

own, and that helps me figure out if the size I've selected will give me the look I want.

To get a little more into it: Finished measurements include a pattern's ease, which is the additional room included in a pattern on top of your body measurements. But ease isn't just included for comfort (this type of ease is called "wearing ease"). It's also included for the style of the garment (called "design ease"). A dress meant to pull on over your head (like the Chemise Dress or the Popover Dress) will necessarily have much more ease than a very fitted dress with a zipper (like the Boatneck Dress).

So while two dresses may technically be the same size, their finished dimensions may be different based on the specific amount of ease factored in for each one's design. A caftan in a

Blousy dress

the pattern is drafted for a non-stretch woven. As every fabric is different (and can contain different percentages of spandex), there's no absolute formula for deciding how much width to remove. That's where a basted fitting comes in handy: Baste the side seams using a long machine stitch to check if you need to remove more width. This should be done with a pattern that you already know fits you well in a non-stretch fabric. For instance, you'd first want to make a test version (or muslin, see page 73) in a non-stretch fabric and perfect the fit. Once you know the pattern fits you well, you can try it in a stretch woven, using a basted fitting to check the ease during garment construction.

Fitted dress

size 6 will look a lot different than a wiggle dress in a size 6! Both are drafted to fit the same measurements but with different amounts of design ease.

Keep in mind, too, that stretch fabric affects the amount of ease needed in a garment. So many wovens contain stretch fibers these days, and some of them contain a lot of it! Spandex (also called elastane) woven into a fabric means that the garment can have much less wearing ease, as it conforms to the body and moves with you. Keep this in mind if you're measuring a garment with stretch to get its finished measurements, or if you're planning a dress in a stretch woven. My strategy is usually to remove a bit of width from the side seams (see page 74) when making a dress in a stretch woven if

Start with Your Measurements

Start by taking your own measurements at the bust, high bust, waist, and hip. Wear foundation garments that fit well (even better if they are the foundations you plan to wear with the dress; this is especially important when planning to wear waist cinchers, merry widows, and bustiers under a dress, because they change your measurements by reshaping your body). When measuring, stand up straight, keep your legs together, and always hold the tape straight and parallel to the floor.

BUST: Take this measurement around the fullest part of the bust, from front to back. Double check that your tape measure is straight across the back and across the breasts.

HIGH BUST: This measurement can be helpful if you are especially large- or small-busted. In those cases, if you choose a pattern size based on your full bust, you can end up with a garment that is either way too small or too large in the shoulders. The high bust (when compared with the full bust) can be a good indicator of whether or not you need a full or small bust adjustment. (See more info in the box on page 72.)

WAIST: This is usually the narrowest part of your torso, but not always. I will tell you now that your natural waist is probably higher than you think it is! Do the "I'm a Little Teapot" dance move, bending your torso over to one side. Where your side creases as you bend is your natural waist. I know a lot of women prefer to wear their waistlines lower, and many ready-to-wear garments sit lower, but for '50s styles, it is most flattering to have the waistline of a garment sit at your natural waist.

HIPS: The widest part of your lower body, this is your lower hip (around the backside) rather than your upper hip (where your actual hip

bone is). I take my hip measurement around the rear end, and over the crotch in the front. This one is probably lower than you think! If you are especially curvy or fleshy in the lower body, it can help to take this measurement while seated, as the body tends to spread a bit in a sitting position.

Once you have these three measurements, compare them to the size chart and see where you fall.

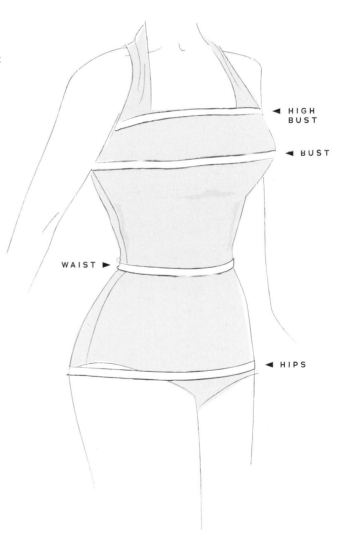

GRADING UP OR DOWN IN SIZE

Use the nested lines to grade up or down.

How to Choose a Size

My first piece of advice is: Don't go by your waist size! Ladies with a larger waist often think they need a bigger pattern and will choose a size based on their waist measurement. Unfortunately, this usually means that the bust and shoulder end up being too large. It's better to go by your high bust or full bust measurement, and then adjust the waist as needed (more on that soon) because the bust and shoulders are the most difficult areas of the body to fit. Based on your bust, waist, and hip measurements, you may fit more than one pattern size, which means that you will need to grade between sizes (see below).

Note that when a dress has a very full skirt, there's no need to worry about your hip measurement.

GRADING BETWEEN SIZES

Modern patterns (and the patterns included in this book) are multi-sized patterns, meaning that several sizes are "nested" inside each other. This is awesome news if your measurements mean that you fall into a couple of different sizes. So if you're a size 12 in the waist and a 14 in the hips, all you have to do is gradually angle out from the 12 at the waistline and taper into the 14 at the full hip line.

GRADING UP OR DOWN IN SIZE

You can also use a multisize pattern to grade up or down to sizes that aren't included with the pattern, if you are smaller or larger than either end of the pattern's size range. Use a ruler to measure the difference between sizes, and incrementally increase or decrease the pattern accordingly. You'll have to measure the difference every few inches or so along the pattern's outline because it can change throughout the pattern. (For instance, the difference between sizes isn't so pronounced in the armhole as it is in the waist or hips.) Increase or decrease the pattern one size at a time until you reach the size you need.

Making a Muslin

To figure out what pattern adjustments may need to be made, and to test the fit of a garment, it's a great idea to make a muslin mock-up. Muslin is an inexpensive unbleached cotton that makes it really easy to see fit issues when basted together and tried on.

To make a muslin, cut out the crucial pieces from muslin fabric. The main pattern pieces are sufficient for a muslin. You don't need to include facings or pockets, unless you think you might need to make a major change to them or want to practice sewing the garment completely together before sewing the actual fabric. If your dress has a waistline seam (like the Boatneck Dress), you can also just make a muslin of the bodice, as skirt adjustments are often easier and may just involve adding or removing width or length.

Sew the muslin using a contrasting thread color (this makes it easier to see the staystitching from the right side of the muslin). First stitch any darts, seamlines, or princess seams using a long machine stitch (a long stitch makes it easier to remove for adjustments). Then stitch the bodice front to the bodice back at the shoulders and side seams. Leave the back open, if there's a zipper opening. I usually baste a lapped zipper

(see page 51) into my bodice muslins, which makes it easier to close than pinning, especially when you're fitting yourself.

Staystitch around the neckline, waistline, and armholes. This just means to sew a line of stitches at $5/8$" from the cut edge so that you can clearly see where the seam lines are when you try on the muslin.

Try on your muslin wearing the undergarments you plan to wear with the dress, and pin or zip the zipper opening closed (if applicable). Take a while to look in the mirror and evaluate the fit. Is the bodice too short or long in any area? See the section on length adjustments. Too tight or loose? Check out the width adjustments section. If it's too large or small in the bust, you'll need to make a (you guessed it) bust adjustment. Also look for gaping armholes and necklines and see if any adjustments need to be made. See the next section for the most common adjustments.

The muslin stage is a great time to ask for fitting advice from a friend or teacher with experience. Or post pictures to a closed Facebook group (there's one specifically for Gertie patterns!) to get help from virtual sewing friends all over the world.

Adjusting Your Patterns

WIDTH ADJUSTMENTS

It's easy to add or remove width as needed to a pattern. One of the more common adjustments I see when I'm teaching is needing to add width to the waist. As mentioned earlier, it's best to choose a pattern size by your bust and then add to the waist as needed.

Adding width at the side seams is the simplest way for making small width adjustments. First, take into account how much you need to

gain in the waist (or wherever you are adding width). Let's say it's 2" (5 cm). Divide that number by 4 (the number of seam allowances at the side seams: the front and the back, on two sides of the body). So to gain 2", you need to add ½" (1.3 cm) at each side seam.

Make a mark ½" (1.3 cm) outside the side seam cutting line at the waistline level. Extend the waistline so that it meets this mark (if your dress has a waistline seam, i.e., the bodice and skirt are cut separately). Next, use your ruler to draw a diagonal line from the original underarm cutting line to the next waistline mark. Repeat for the back pattern piece. If your dress does not have a waistline seam (bodice and skirt are cut in one piece), extend the line for the new width all the way down to the hipline to gain width in the hips as well, or taper back to your original size at the hips if you do not need additional width in the hips. If the side seam is straight, you'll just be drawing a straight line, but if it's at all curved, you should replicate the curve in your new line.

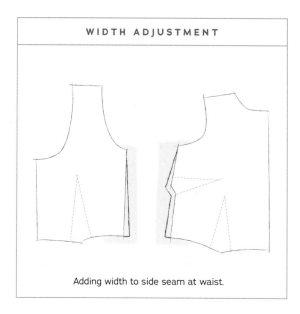

WIDTH ADJUSTMENT

Adding width to side seam at waist.

Removing width works the same way, but in reverse.

But what do you do if your dress pattern has a bust dart? First, close the dart and pin it as it would be sewn, with the dart excess (the folded part) under the pattern and pressed down toward the waist. Now that the dart is closed, you have a straight edge at the side seam, making it easier to add width as described above. After you have a new side seam line, you need to true the dart (see the box at right).

TRUEING A DART

Trueing a dart is one of those techniques that always impresses students when I demonstrate it, because it seems a little like magic! When you change a seamline with a dart, such as a side seam or a waist seam, you need to redraw the dart base (that pointy bit that comes out from the dart) so that the cutting line is accurate. First, close the dart and pin it so that the lines are matching. Fold the dart excess so that it faces down (for horizontal darts) or toward center back or center front, respectively (for vertical darts). Use a spoked tracing wheel to trace the new line, preferably with corkboard underneath your pattern paper (A). When you unfold the dart, the new cutting lines are magically there! Draw over the perforations with pencil (B).

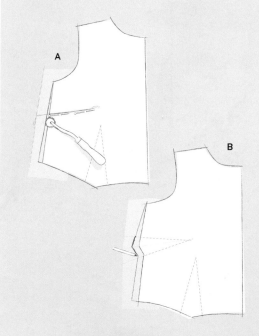

A. Close dart and trace over new seam.
B. Open dart and draw over traced lines.

LENGTH ADJUSTMENTS

If you're petite or short-waisted, you may find that you often have excess length in your bodices, which shows up in the form of horizontal folds of fabric. This problem is easy to fix on a pattern. Make a horizontal slash in the pattern piece from the side-seam cutting line to the center-front or -back cutting line or foldline and overlap the two pieces by the amount you want to shorten the bodice. Don't forget to redraw (true) the side-seam cutting lines to make them smooth again. If the slash intersected a dart, redraw the dart legs. You can apply this slash-and-overlap method anywhere you need to remove extra length from a dress, including the skirt (just take the tuck between the hipline and the knees). You can also remove length from the bottom of a skirt.

If you are tall or long-waisted, you may have the opposite problem: too little length in a bodice. You can apply the same principle, but instead of slashing and overlapping, you slash and spread. Cut the pattern and then spread the pieces apart the amount of length you need to add. Tape new paper behind the slash and redraw the cutting lines and darts.

Swayback Adjustment

Sometimes you have to make a length adjustment that does not go all the way across a pattern piece. The swayback adjustment is a great example of this. A person is said to be "swaybacked" if she has a lower back that curves in considerably. This is often seen in conjunction with a round derriere. You'll know you need a swayback adjustment if you see extra fabric pooling around your lower back on a muslin or dress; this often looks like horizontal folds.

To fix this, take a tuck in the muslin to remove that extra fabric. Start in the middle of the lower back, pinching out the full amount needed. Taper this tuck toward the side seams, so that it reduces to nothing. In other words, it's a wedge-shaped tuck. Transfer the tuck to

LENGTH ADJUSTMENTS

Slash and spread to add length to a bodice.

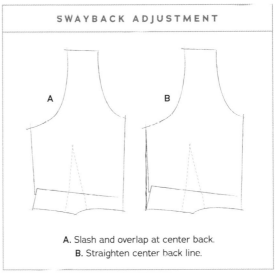

SWAYBACK ADJUSTMENT

A

B

A. Slash and overlap at center back.
B. Straighten center back line.

your pattern. You'll most likely be working on a half-pattern piece. Make a horizontal slash at the waistline on the back pattern piece, but leave a tiny bit of pattern connected at the side-seam cutting line (this is often called a "hinge" in pattern adjustment lingo). Overlap the slashed edges by the amount you want to take out of the lower back. After overlapping, you will notice that the center back line is now crooked. Use a ruler to straighten out the line from neck to waist.

FULL BUST ADJUSTMENTS

Full bust adjustments are such a common alteration! I've seen several methods of doing it, but this one makes the most sense to me. You'll be adding both length and width to accommodate a fuller bust. Note I'm showing this method on a traditional darted bodice with a waist seam, so that you can see the basic principle. Different pattern styles require different adjustments, but the principle is the same: adding both length and width.

It helps to know how much width and length you need to add. Start by making a muslin. Slash into it horizontally and vertically, with the lines crossing at the full bust line. Let the muslin slashes expand as much as you need for the bodice to sit without pulling and place some muslin scraps behind the slashes, pinning them to secure. Measure the length and width of your patched-in scrap fabric. These are the amounts you need to add to the pattern horizontally and vertically.

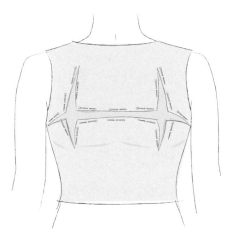

Slash and patch your muslin to determine how much to add at bust.

Now that you know how much extra room you need, go to your paper pattern. You're going to make three lines on the pattern:

1. Draw a horizontal line from the side seam through the bust dart, ending at the bust apex.

2. Draw a vertical line through the waistline dart to the bust apex. Extend it from the bust apex to the middle of the armhole in a diagonal line.

3. Draw a horizontal line from the vertical line to the bodice center front, half the distance between the bust and the waist (A).

4. Now slash through the horizontal line at the bust. Next, slash into the vertical line and along the diagonal line, leaving a hinge at the armhole. Finally, slash through the second horizontal line, cutting all the way through the pattern piece.

5. Expand the slashes at the bust dart and waist dart by the amount of the needed addition, using your patched muslin measurement. Move the piece below the third slash down until it matches the waistline at the side seam (B). You may have noticed that you've expanded the darts. That's okay! You're going to use the original darts lines to make new, deeper darts. Curvier figures need deep darts; the adjusted front pattern will still fit into the other adjacent pieces.

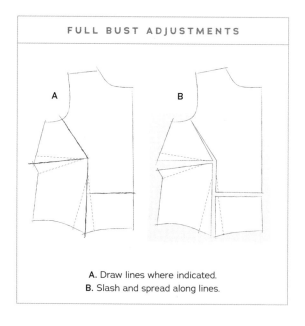

FULL BUST ADJUSTMENTS

A

B

A. Draw lines where indicated.
B. Slash and spread along lines.

SMALL BUST ADJUSTMENTS

This is the opposite of a full bust adjustment, so you just need to do the opposite steps to those at left. When trying on your muslin, figure out how much length and width you need to remove by taking tucks vertically and horizontally. Then follow the full bust adjustment instructions, overlapping your pattern pieces rather than spreading them.

GAPING NECKLINE

Take tiny tucks to remove gaping.

SMALL BUST ADJUSTMENTS

Slash and overlap along indicated lines.

GAPING NECKLINE

You can take tiny little tucks in a pattern's neckline to remove gaping. Tape down the pattern tucks so that they are flat, which will remove excess fabric from the neckline when you cut it out.

NARROW SHOULDER

If your dress sits too far out past your shoulder rather than ending directly on your shoulder bone, you probably have a narrow shoulder. With your muslin on, mark where you want your shoulder point to sit. (Make sure to take into account the seam allowance; this is why I always staystitch my seam lines in a muslin.) Make the

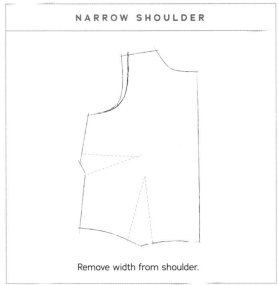

NARROW SHOULDER

Remove width from shoulder.

pattern alteration by redrawing the armhole so that the shoulder is narrower, tapering it to the original underarm curve.

These are just some of the most common adjustments I see when fitting students. There is a whole world of knowledge to be gained by fitting yourself and others, and also by reading up on the topic. See Resources (page 138) for some of my favorite fitting books.

Foundation Garments

It's no secret that I love lingerie, particularly vintage-style foundation garments. In fact, I do a whole series on social media showing a dress and the underwear I wear with it. Yep, underwear pictures on the Internet! (My mom is so proud.) The reason I'm committed to this series is that the right foundation garments totally change the look and fit of a dress. I don't wear shapewear every day, but when I do, I am so much happier with the fit and silhouette of a garment. The '50s especially were all about defined waists, perky busts, and curvy hips. No matter what your body proportions, trying out some shapewear can give you a lovely retro silhouette under your dresses and make you feel just a little more fabulous!

Here are a few of my favorite vintage-style foundation garments:

MERRY WIDOW: This is a longline strapless bra that comes down to the upper hip. It cinches your waist with steel boning and gives lift to the bust. My favorite is from What Katie Did, a fabulous London brand that makes reproduction vintage lingerie. I wear mine with strappy and strapless dresses, and anything with a wide-set neckline.

LONGLINE BRA: This is a regular bra (with straps) that ends at the waist. It often has steel boning and seamed cups for a perky uplifted shape. I love my front-closure Carnival 745: it gives amazing waist definition and a fabulous retro silhouette to the bust. Wear a longline bra with high-waisted panties so you don't have a gap between your bra and knickers!

LONGLINE GIRDLE: A girdle is your best friend if you're wearing a tight skirt! These look like bike shorts, coming up to the natural waist and ending below the thigh. Spanx is the modern-day equivalent, but I prefer old-school styles from Rago, a company that's been selling classic shapewear for decades. A girdle is great with a longline bra, giving you a cinched and smooth look all over (no panty lines!).

WAIST CINCHER: If you have a hard-to-find bra size (and can't find a good longline bra or merry widow to fit), a great solution is a waist cincher worn with a bra you already own. A waist cincher is a boned garment made from powermesh for your midriff (the area from the underbust to the upper hip) that has a front hook-and-eye closure. It often has

Underbust corset

Merry widow

Longline bra

garters attached (ooh la la, don't even get me started on stockings!). A waist cincher does just what it says, pulling in your waist for a little extra definition while allowing you to wear your preferred bra.

CORSET: When you want a super-cinched waist in a dress, call in the big guns: corsetry! I love an underbust corset for special occasions and photo shoots (yes, I'm wearing one in many of the photos in this book) because it is amazingly transformative. When you get fitted for your first corset, you won't believe the wasp-waisted creature you see in the mirror! My favorite underbust corset is a waist cincher by Dark Garden in San Francisco, made in pink silk satin with a special busk cover in the front to eliminate bumps from the post-and-eye closure (what's called a "busk").

PETTICOAT: It's not exactly shapewear, but a petticoat will totally transform the look of a dress as well. For full skirts, a petticoat will make your dress stand out in a fabulous way. I have two levels of petticoatedness (yes, that's a word, I swear): everyday and extreme. My everyday petticoat is a light chiffon number by Malco Modes (a style named "Zooey"). For special occasions, I wear their much fuller chiffon petticoat (a style named "Samantha"). You want your petticoat to be about an inch shorter than your dress, so you may need a couple of different styles and lengths (and colors, of course!).

PART TWO

Wardrobe

Now that you've studied the techniques involved in simple dressmaking, it's time to put them to practice making a fab wardrobe of dresses! There are five patterns included in this book, but I show you one or two variations on each of them, making for twelve lovely frocks.

About the Patterns

The five dress patterns come on sturdy, double-sided paper sheets in the included envelope in the back of the book. Each pattern piece is nested in all eight sizes (see the next section for information on sizing), so the sizes sit inside each other like Russian dolls. Some of the pattern pieces overlap each other for space reasons, so keep that in mind as you're identifying your pieces.

To use the patterns, trace the pieces you want (see pages 134–136). Use clean pattern paper, butcher paper, medical paper, or Swedish tracing paper—whatever works for you! My favorite way to trace patterns is to use a large corkboard and place my clean paper on top of it. Then put the pattern sheet on top of that and use a spiky tracing wheel to trace around the lines of the pattern. Because the corkboard's surface has some give, the wheel will leave easily discernible holes for you to connect with a ruler and pencil when you lift away the pattern sheet. I find this way easy because I don't have to worry about squinting through the clean paper!

Don't forget to transfer all the pattern marks, like the grainlines, notches, circles, and darts. Also make sure to label each pattern piece clearly with the name and the size you traced—this will help you refer back to the pattern pieces easily (and avoid having those pesky "mystery paper pieces" that end up in the trash after all your hard work tracing!). I store all my pattern pieces in large manila envelopes and label them clearly on the outside.

I urge you to take these patterns to the next level: What kind of variations would you have designed? A pattern is just a template for your creativity, and there are no limits to what you can do by combining different trims and other elements.

Seam Allowances

All pattern pieces include a ⅝" (1.5 cm) seam allowance, except where noted otherwise. In some cases, like the long tie piece on the Swirl Dress (page 107), I use a ¼" (6 mm) seam allowance as it avoids having to trim down that long seam allowance before turning the piece right side out. When a ¼" (6 mm) seam allowance is used, it's noted in the dress instructions.

SIZE CHART

	2	4	6	8	10	12	14	16
Bust	32" 81.3 cm	34" 86.4 cm	36" 91.4 cm	38" 96.5 cm	40" 101.6 cm	42" 106.7 cm	44" 111.8 cm	46" 116.8 cm
Waist	24" 61 cm	26" 66 cm	28" 71.1 cm	30" 76.2 cm	32" 81.3 cm	34" 86.4 cm	36" 91.4 cm	38" 96.5 cm
Hips	36" 91.4 cm	38" 96.5 cm	40" 101.6 cm	42" 106.7 cm	44" 111.8 cm	46" 116.8 cm	48" 121.9 cm	50" 127 cm

Sizing

The patterns come in sizes 2 through 16. Please note that this is my own sizing system (the same that I've used in all my previous books and in my independent pattern line, Charm Patterns) and it is very similar to American ready-to-wear sizes. However, my sizing tends to be more generous in the bust and hip than other systems. So please measure yourself and check the size chart before deciding on a size! There are also finished garment measurements for each of the dress patterns on page 137, and that's another piece of important information to help you decide on a size. Please consult chapter seven for more detailed information on measuring yourself, how to choose a size, and how to make basic pattern adjustments.

Note that when tracing your patterns, you may wish to grade between two sizes. For instance, you may be a size 12 at the waist, but a size 14 in the hips. It's really simple to draw a line that starts at the 12 at the waist, and then gradually taper the line out to the 14 at the hips. It's incredibly rare for any woman to exactly conform to just one size on the chart. Sewing is about making the clothes conform to you, not vice versa! So don't be put off if you need to do a little melding of sizes to get the patterns to work for you: Getting a custom fit is part of what makes sewing so satisfying.

The Popover Dress

I named this dress as an homage to Clare McCardell, a '50s designer who was a master of the chic "throw on and go" frock. Please don't be put off by its voluminous shape! It's intended to be cinched at the waist with a purchased belt, giving it that fabulous fit-and-flare silhouette.

This is the easiest dress in the book, as it has only one main pattern piece. You can make this dress even simpler by omitting the shoulder bows and flap-patch pockets. Complete the cut-on neck facing, sew a few seams and a hem, bind the armholes, and you're done! Or take it to the next level by cutting it on the bias in a plaid, check, or stripe pattern to get a chevron effect. You can even try using elastic shirring around the midriff for a stretchy but shapely look, as in the second variation.

Another idea: Try shortening it to mini length and sewing it as a '60s-style shift or little baby-doll nightie, perhaps with a ruffle around the hem! The trapeze shape will work perfectly in that case, no cinching required.

My first version is in a bandana-print quilting cotton. This design works well in most cottons (including quilting cottons, sateen, lawn, and gingham), as well as linen and rayon wovens.

SUPPLIES

- 3⅓ yards (3 m) 45"- (114 cm-) or 2⅝ yards (2.4 m) 60"- (152 cm-) wide fabric
- Strips of 1¼"- (3.2 cm-) wide fusible interfacing to stabilize neckline (about 1 yard [0.9 m] long)
- Thread to match fabric

SKILLS

- Cut-on facing (page 46)
- Staystitching (page 35)
- Seams (page 39)
- Pivoting (page 39)
- Stitching in the ditch (page 47)
- Bias facings (page 48)
- Understitching (page 47)
- Narrow hem (page 56)
- Patch pockets (page 62)

PATTERN PIECES

Pattern sheet 1, following layout on page 134.
1. Dress front and back (cut 4, fabric)
2. Armhole bias facings (cut 2, fabric)
3. Pocket (cut 2, fabric)
4. Pocket facing (cut 2, fabric)
5. Shoulder bow (cut 4, fabric)

A. Serge edges.

B. Apply interfacing.

C. Staystitch neckline.

D. Stitch center seams.

E. Stitch side and shoulder seams.

F. Sew armhole facing.

H. Stitch around bow.

G. Sew pockets.

INSTRUCTIONS

1. After cutting the pattern pieces following the layout on page 134, transfer markings (pocket placements and the circle at the V-neck) and clip into any notches.

2. If you are serge-finishing the raw edges, serge all the vertical seam allowances and the outer edge of the cut-on facing (A).

3. Apply strips of 1¼"- (3.2 cm-) wide fusible interfacing to the cut-on facing's wrong side (B).

4. Staystitch the cut-on facing's fold line (see page 35), next to the edge of the fused interfacing, from the shoulder seam to the pivot-point circle at the neckline (C).

5. Pin one set of front/back dress pieces right sides together at the center-front/center-back seam. Stitch the seam from bottom to top, and then pivot the stitching at the facing's inner corner (see page 39). Press the seam allowances open. Repeat with the second set of dress pieces. One set is the dress front and one is the dress back (D).

6. Pin the dress front to the dress back at the side seams and shoulders, right sides together, and stitch. Press the seam allowances open (E).

7. Press the cut-on neckline facing to the wrong side of the dress and pin it in place at the shoulder seams and the center-front/center-back necklines. Stitch in the ditches of the seams to secure the facings in place (see page 47).

8. Form each bias armhole facing into a ring by pinning the short ends' right sides together and stitching. Press the seam allowances open. Pin each facing to each dress armhole's right side, matching seams to the bodice side seams and the notches to the shoulder seams. Stitch using a ⅝" (1.5 cm) seam allowance. To understitch the facings (see page 47), turn them over the seam allowances and stitch next to the seam, catching seam allowances underneath. Turn the facing and seam allowances to the

Belted

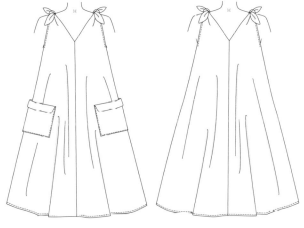

Unbelted

wrong side of the dress and fold the raw edge under so the facing is doubled. Press in place and then topstitch around the armhole (see page 41), securing the facing (F).

9. Hang the dress overnight to allow the bias to stretch. Even the hem by measuring up from the floor, marking, and trimming.

10. Sew a narrow hem (see page 56).

11. Optional pockets: Finish the lower edges of the pocket facings by serging, pinking, zigzagging, or turning under ¼" (6 mm) and topstitching. Pin the pocket facings to the pockets, right sides together. Stitch all the way around the pockets at ⅝" (1.5 cm). Trim the pocket flap seam allowances and turn right side out. Finish around the rest of the pockets using the method of your choice (see page 40). Press under the seam allowances so that the ⅝" (1.5 cm) stitching is rolled to the wrong side. Press the whole pocket flat. Pin the pockets to the dress, matching the markings. Edgestitch the pockets in place (see page 41), starting and ending at the circle marks, leaving the pocket flaps free (G).

12. Optional shoulder bows: Pin a set of two shoulder bow pieces right sides together. Stitch around all sides, using a ¼" (6 mm) seam allowance and leaving 1"- (2.5 cm-) long openings for turning. Turn the bows right side out and press. Edgestitch the openings closed. Tie into a knot around each shoulder of the dress (H).

Bias-Cut with Waistline Shirring

Cutting this dress on the bias in a plaid, check, or stripe pattern gives it a totally different look! Be warned, though: You do need to cut the fabric so that its pattern matches at center front and back, giving it that pleasing chevron effect at the seams. The best way to do this is to cut each piece individually, and mark on the pattern piece where one of the major lines of the fabric's pattern should appear. Cut each piece, checking that the line matches the pattern mark. As you sew the seams, double-check that the plaid/check/stripe is correctly aligned.

When fabric is cut on the bias, a lot more stretching can occur when you hang the dress overnight. I made this version in a lovely gingham cotton gauze, which is very loosely woven. Because of the loose weave, the fabric stretched even more than usual on the bias—8" (20 cm) in some places! This resulted in the entire dress stretching out and becoming longer and narrower, so this version has a more streamlined look.

Besides cutting the dress on the bias, the other change I made was to add elastic shirring around the waist for a comfy but cinched look. For more information on elastic shirring, see page 43.

SUPPLIES

- 3⅝ yards (3.3 m) 45"- (114 cm-) or 2¾ yards (2.5 m) 60"- (152 cm-) wide fabric
- "Hera" marker (optional)
- Strips of 1¼"- (3.2 cm-) wide fusible interfacing to stabilize neckline (about 1 yard [0.9 m] long)
- Thread to match fabric
- 2 spools elastic shirring thread

Stitch shirring in a spiral pattern.

1. After cutting the pattern pieces following the layout on page 134, transfer markings and clip into any notches. Be sure to transfer the elastic shirring mark on the pattern to the right side of all the cut pieces. One easy and nonpermanent way to mark these lines on the outside of the dress is to use a "Hera" marker, a tool that transfers lines by softly creasing the fabric. Then you follow the creases as the stitching lines. (Alternatively, you can try on the dress mid-construction and decide where you want the shirring to start.)

2. Follow steps 2–8 of the Popover Dress instructions. After completing step 8, wind elastic thread onto a bobbin (see pages 43) and begin stitching along the marked shirring placement line at a side seam, backstitching first. As your stitches approach the starting point again, instead of meeting the previous line of stitching, gradually steer the garment ¼" (6 mm) below the first line of stitching to apply the elastic thread in a spiral pattern. Continue in this way until you've stitched about 4½" (11.5 cm) deep around the midriff. You will probably need to start a new bobbin at some point, so just backstitch or pull both threads to the inside of the dress and tie them in a knot. Backstitch at the end of the shirring. Steam the shirring from the inside to shrink it back to its original length (A).

3. Finish the dress following steps 9–12 in the Popover Dress instructions, omitting the pockets and shoulder bows, or add them if you like—they'd be super cute on this version as well!

Inside view of shirred dress

The Chemise Dress

The chemise dress was a sort of '50s precursor to the '60s shift dress (though the name comes from the chemise undergarment that was worn under corsets in Victorian times). Much like the Popover Dress (page 85), this is a simple-to-sew frock with no closures that looks most flattering when cinched in various ways at the waist. In this first version, I created an interior casing and then threaded elastic through it for a comfortable but shapely silhouette. You'll see two other creative options for cinching in the following variations, and I'm sure you can think of many more!

The skirt is slightly tapered at the knee and has a slit in the back for walking ease. The neat bodice finishing is done with an all-in-one facing, which finishes the neckline and the armholes simultaneously.

I made this version in rayon challis (one of my own fabric designs with little roses and berries!), which is a great fabric when you're looking for something to drape over the body, rather than stand away from it. See more about rayon fabric on page 24. This dress style works best in fabrics that have good drape and a soft hand, such as rayon challis or crepe, lightweight cotton, and wool and silk crepe wovens.

SUPPLIES

- 2½ yards (2.3 m) 45"- (114 cm-) or 1¾ yards (1.6 m) 60"- (152 cm-) wide fabric
- 1 yard (.9 m) 20"- (52 cm-) wide fusible interfacing
- Thread to match fabric
- About 2 yards (1.8 m) of ½"- (1.3 cm-) wide single-fold bias tape
- 1 yard (0.9 m) of ¼"- (6 mm-) wide braided elastic
- Small safety pin

SKILLS

- Staystitching (page 35)
- Seams (page 39)
- Darts (page 38)
- Grading and clipping (page 46)
- Understitching (page 47)
- Stitching in the ditch (page 47)
- Edgestitching (page 41)

PATTERN PIECES

Pattern sheet 2, following layout on page 134.
1. Dress front (cut 1 on fold, fabric)
2. Dress back (cut 2, fabric)
3. Front facing (cut 1 on fold, fabric and interfacing)
4. Back facing (cut 2, fabric and interfacing)

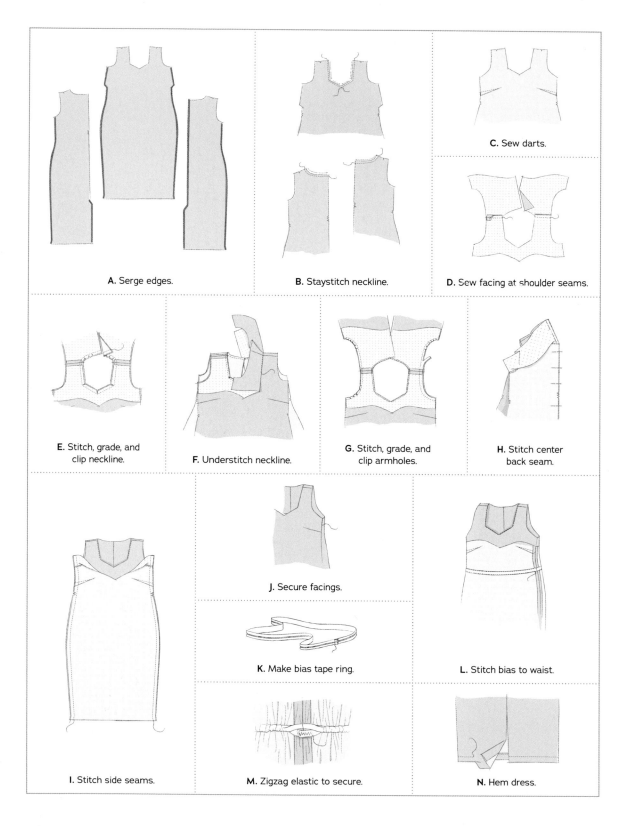

A. Serge edges.

B. Staystitch neckline.

C. Sew darts.

D. Sew facing at shoulder seams.

E. Stitch, grade, and clip neckline.

F. Understitch neckline.

G. Stitch, grade, and clip armholes.

H. Stitch center back seam.

I. Stitch side seams.

J. Secure facings.

K. Make bias tape ring.

L. Stitch bias to waist.

M. Zigzag elastic to secure.

N. Hem dress.

INSTRUCTIONS

1. After cutting the pattern pieces following the layout on page 134, transfer markings (darts, elastic casing line, and back slit markings) and clip into any notches.

2. If you are serge-finishing the raw edges (see page 35), serge all the vertical seam allowances and the vertical edge of the back slit extension (A).

3. Apply the fusible interfacing to the wrong sides of their corresponding facings, following the instructions on page 34. Finish the lower edges of the front and back facings using the method of your choice (see page 47).

4. Staystitch around the front and back neckline (see page 35) (B).

5. Sew the bust darts on the dress front (see page 38). Press the darts toward the waist (C).

6. Pin the dress front to the dress backs at the shoulders, right sides together. Stitch and press the seam allowances open.

7. Pin the dress front facing to the dress back facings at the shoulders, right sides together. Stitch, and press the seam allowances open (D).

8. Pin the facing unit to the dress unit around the neckline, right sides together. Stitch around the three pivot points of the sweetheart neckline by stopping with your needle down, lifting the presser foot, and changing direction. (It can be helpful to mark in the seam allowances around the sweetheart neckline to identify the pivot points.) Clip into the three pivot points as close as possible to the stitching without cutting through it. Grade the neckline seam allowances, remembering that the dress seam allowance should be the wider one. Clip into the inner curves of the back neckline (see page 46) (E).

9. Turn the facing over the neckline seam allowances and understitch, catching the seam allowances in the stitching (see page 47) (F).

10. Turn the facing back so that the dress and facing are right sides together again. Pin the facing to the dress around the armholes, matching the shoulder seams. Stitch around each armhole. Grade the armhole seam allowances, remembering that the dress seam allowance should be the wider one (see page 46). Clip into the inner curves of the armholes (G).

11. Turn the dress right side out by reaching through each shoulder and pulling the dress to the right side.

12. Understitch the armholes as far as possible up to the shoulder seam; you will have to understitch each armhole in two separate stages.

13. Press the dress neckline and armholes, rolling the understitching to the wrong side. Pin the center-back seam of the dress right sides together from the hem up to the facing, with the facing flipped away from the dress (H).

14. Stitch from the top of the facing down to the slit circle mark. When you reach the circle, backstitch and change the stitch length to the longest setting. Baste the slit opening closed from the mark to the hem. Press the center-back seam allowances open and turn the facing to the wrong side of the dress.

15. Pin the dress front to the back at the side seams, right sides together, from the hem up to the facing, with the facing flipped away from the dress. Stitch from the top of the facing to the hem. Press the seam allowances open and turn the facing to the inside of the dress (I).

16. Secure the facings at the side seams and the center-back seam by stitching in the ditch (see page 47) (J).

17. Cut a piece of bias tape the length of the elastic casing line on the patten plus ½" (1.3 cm). Form the bias tape into a ring by sewing it at the short ends, right sides together, with a ¼" (6 mm) seam allowance. Press the seam allowances open (K).

18. Align the top edge of the bias tape ring to the elastic casing line and pin in place around the waistline on the dress's wrong side. Edgestitch along the upper edge of the bias tape (see page 41). Repeat edgestitching along lower edge of bias tape, leaving a ½" (1.3 cm) opening in the stitching to feed the elastic into (L).

19. Cut a length of elastic that fits very snugly stretched around your waist, plus 1" (2.5 cm) for an overlap.

20. Attach a safety pin to one end of the elastic and thread it carefully through the casing, making sure not to twist the elastic. It's a good idea to secure the loose end to the fabric with a pin. Be extra careful at the intersecting seams; it may take a few tries to find the right path for the elastic through the layers. Once the elastic is fully threaded, overlap the ends of the elastic by ½" (1.3 cm) and pin them together. Pull the elastic out of the casing enough so that you can place it under your sewing machine's presser foot. Using a 2.5-mm-wide zigzag stitch, sew through the overlapped ends (M).

21. Distribute the gathers around the waistline. With a straight stitch, sew the opening in the casing closed, backstitching at each end.

22. Remove the basting from the back slit of the dress.

23. Finish the raw edge of the dress hem using the method of your choice. With the back slit extensions still pressed under, press the hem under by 1¼" (3.2 cm) and topstitch in place 1" (2.5 cm) from the bottom of the hem (N).

Inside view of Chemise Dress

Square Neckline with Belt

I made this version in a lightweight linen/rayon blend, which has a lovely drape. I did some very simple pattern modifications to change the neckline from a sweetheart shape to a square. To cinch the waist, I made a fabric belt that attaches to two buttons at the front waistline. I love the chic silhouette this creates.

SUPPLIES

- 2½ yards (2.3 m) 45"- (114 cm-) or 1¾ yards (1.6 m) 60"- (152 cm-) wide fabric
- 1 yard (.9 m) 20"- (52 cm-) wide fusible interfacing
- Thread to match fabric
- 2 large buttons

INSTRUCTIONS

1. When tracing the pattern pieces, trace the dress front and facing front pieces, but do not cut out around the neckline yet. Using a clear gridded ruler, place the ruler at a 90-degree angle to the lowest point of the sweetheart neckline at center front. Draw a line from this point to the shoulder strap. Extend the shoulder strap neckline edge to meet the line you just drew. You now have a square neckline! Repeat this process on the front facing. Extend and reshape the bottom of the neckline facing so that it is at least 2" (5 cm) wide at all points (A).

2. Cut out the dress and interfacing as usual, and transfer the button markings and back slit marking, as well as any notches.

3. Construct the dress following steps 2–16 in the Chemise Dress instructions.

4. Sew the two buttons in place by hand at the button marks on the dress. Anchor the thread on the fabric's wrong side and then come up and down through the button's holes a few times to secure the button in place (B).

5. Try the dress on and then measure around your waist from button to button, where the belt will sit, pulling the measuring tape comfortably snug but not tight. Cut a 4¾"- (12 cm-) wide rectangle of fabric and interfacing the length of your button-to-button measurement plus 1¼" (3.2 cm). Fuse the interfacing to the rectangle's wrong side. Fold the rectangle in half lengthwise, right sides together, and stitch around all three open edges with a ¼" (6 mm) seam allowance, leaving a 1"- (2.5 cm-) long opening in the middle of the long edge for turning. Snip off the corners of the rectangle and turn right side out. Press the rectangle flat and close the opening with slip-stitching (see page 57).

6. Sew buttonholes on each end of the belt, centering them on the belt ½" (1.3 cm) from the belt ends (see page 54). Attach the belt to one of the buttons on the dress, and then attach the other end after you've put on the dress.

7. Finish the dress by following steps 22 and 23 in the Chemise Dress instructions.

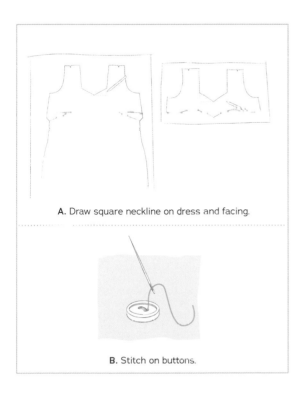

A. Draw square neckline on dress and facing.

B. Stitch on buttons.

Fringe Cocktail Dress

I love fringe! For this evening version of the Chemise Dress, I sewed three rows of fringe to the bottom of the dress. I stitched fringe to each end of a fabric sash and then cinched the dress waist with the sash. This version was made in a rayon challis, which has a beautiful drape; silk or wool crepe would also be lovely.

SUPPLIES

- 2½ yards (2.3 m) 45"- (114 cm-) or 1¾ yards (1.6 m) 60"- (152 cm-) wide fabric
- 1 yard (.9 m) 20"- (52 cm-) wide fusible interfacing
- Thread to match fabric
- 5 yards (4.6 m) of 4"- (10 cm-) long fringe trim

INSTRUCTIONS

1. Follow all the steps except 17–21 (the elastic casing) in the Chemise Dress instructions.

2. After the dress is completed and hemmed, construct the sash. Cut a rectangle 8" (20 cm) wide by 54" (1.4 m) long. Fold the rectangle lengthwise, right sides together, and sew along the three open edges with a ¼" (6 mm) seam allowance, leaving a 3" (7.6 cm) opening in the middle of the long edge for turning. Snip off the corners of the rectangle and turn the sash right side out. Press the rectangle flat and close the opening with slipstitching (see page 57). Wrap fringe around each short end of the sash, turning under the trim's raw edges where they overlap. Pin and edgestitch the fringe in place (A).

3. To attach fringe to the bottom of the dress, first mark a line 2" (5 cm) above the finished hem. Position the fringe so that it just covers the marked line, wrapping the cut trim ends under the back slit opening, and edgestitch the fringe in place. Mark another line 2" (5 cm) above the first row of fringe, and stitch another row of fringe along that line, again wrapping the trim ends under the back slit. Repeat for a third row of fringe (B).

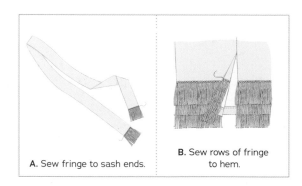

A. Sew fringe to sash ends.

B. Sew rows of fringe to hem.

The Swirl Dress

The Swirl Dress was a very popular style of wrap dress from the '40s through the '60s. It came in adorable novelty-print cottons and was an everyday wardrobe staple. I love the feminine shape of this dress, but what sets it apart is that the bodice is fitted very nicely without the use of darts. The neckline gathers provide the bust shaping. This dress comes together very quickly for that reason. The flared skirt is perfect for every day—not too full and not too slim. Plus, the fact that the dress ties on makes it adjustable! The wrap in the back creates a beautiful V-neck. This dress is lovely with a contrast waist tie, or you can cut the tie from your main fabric.

The Swirl Dress has cut-on kimono sleeves in a short cap length, great for summer or for pairing with a cardigan when the weather gets cooler.

For this version, I used a border print sateen from my fabric line, positioning the large rose border along the hem of the dress. The dress is best in opaque cotton like sateen or shirting, linen, or rayon challis wovens for everyday wear.

SUPPLIES

- 3¼ yards (3 m) 45"- (114 cm-) or 2⅝ yards (2.4 m) 60"- (152 cm-) wide fabric
- 1⅜ yards (1.3 m) contrast fabric for sash (optional)
- 1 yard (.9 m) 20"- (51 cm-) wide fusible interfacing
- Thread to match fabric

SKILLS

- Gathering (page 41)
- Seams (page 39)
- Staystitching (page 35)
- Topstitching (page 41)
- Slipstitching (page 57)
- Pivoting (page 39)
- Neckline facing (page 46)
- Grading and clipping (page 46)
- Understitching (page 47)
- Stitching in the ditch (page 47)
- Narrow hem (page 56)

PATTERN PIECES

Pattern sheet 3 and 4, following layout on page 135.

1. Bodice front (cut 1 on fold, fabric)
2. Bodice back (cut 2, fabric)
3. Front facing (cut 1 on fold, fabric and interfacing)
4. Back facing (cut 2, fabric and interfacing)
5. Sash (cut 2, fabric)
6. Skirt front (cut 1 on fold, fabric)
7. Skirt back (cut 2, fabric)

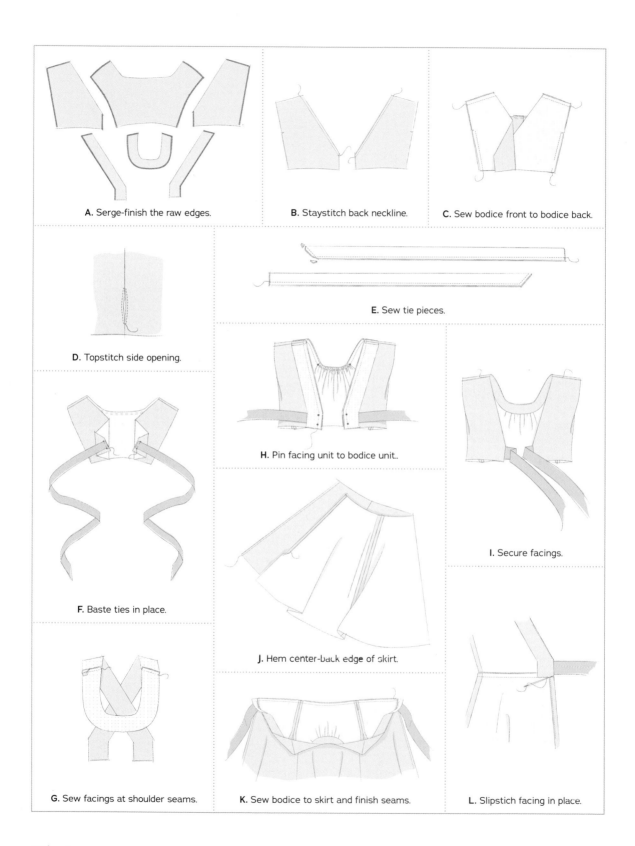

A. Serge-finish the raw edges.

B. Staystitch back neckline.

C. Sew bodice front to bodice back.

D. Topstitch side opening.

E. Sew tie pieces.

F. Baste ties in place.

G. Sew facings at shoulder seams.

H. Pin facing unit to bodice unit..

I. Secure facings.

J. Hem center-back edge of skirt.

K. Sew bodice to skirt and finish seams.

L. Slipstich facing in place.

INSTRUCTIONS

1. After cutting the pattern pieces following the layout on page 135, transfer markings (gathering circles and sash placement circles) and clip into any notches.

2. If you are serge-finishing the raw edges, serge all the vertical seam allowances and the shoulder seam allowances (A).

3. Apply the fusible interfacings to their corresponding facings, following the instructions on page 34. Finish the lower edges of the front and back facings using the method of your choice.

4. Sew gathering stitches between the circles on the bodice front neckline (see page 41).

5. Staystitch the back neckline (see page 35) (B).

6. Sew the bodice front to the bodice back at the shoulder seams, right sides together. Press the seams open.

7. Pin and sew the bodice front to the bodice back at the side seams below the notches, right sides together. Leave the section between the circles unstitched on the left side only, backstitching at each circle (this is for the tie to pass through) (C).

8. Topstitch around the side tie opening (see page 41) at ¼" (6 mm), catching the seam allowances in the stitching (D).

9. Turn under the sleeve seam allowances ⅝" (1.5 cm) and press. Hand-stitch them in place using a slipstitch (see page 57).

10. Sew the tie pieces by folding them in half lengthwise and stitching around the long open side and short angled end with a ¼" (6 mm) seam allowance. Trim off the corners of the sash and turn right side out using a point turner, knitting needle, or chopstick to help you. Press the ties flat (E).

11. Position the ties on the back bodice pieces between the circles, as shown. Baste in place (F).

12. Pin the front facing to the back facings at the shoulder seams, right sides together. Stitch and press the seam allowances open (G).

13. Pin the facing unit to the bodice unit around the neckline, right sides together, pulling up the bodice's gathering stitches so that the gathers are evenly distributed and the front neckline matches the facing at the circles. Stitch, pivoting at the corner above the ties (see page 39) (H).

14. Grade the neckline seam allowances, remembering that the bodice seam allowance should be the wider one. Clip into the inner curves of the front neckline (see page 72) and trim away the corners on the back opening.

15. Understitch the facing around the neckline (see page 47). Press the facing to the wrong side of the bodice.

16. Secure the facings at the shoulder seams by stitching in the ditch (see page 47) (I).

17. Pin the skirt backs to the skirt front at the side seams, right sides together, matching the notches. Stitch, and press the seam allowances open.

18. Turn under each finished center-back edge of the skirt backs by ⅝" (1.5 cm) and press. Topstitch at ½" (1.3 cm) to secure (J).

19. Pin the bodice to the skirt, with right sides together and while matching the side seams. To avoid catching the bodice back facings in the waistline seam, turn the facings out, away from the bodice. Stitch. Finish the waistline seam allowances as one, trimming to ⅜" (1 cm), and press them toward the bodice (K).

20. Turn the back facings to the wrong side of the bodice and fold the lower edge under by ⅝" (1.5 cm). Pin the folded edge in place so that it covers the waistline seam and slipstitch in place (see page 57) (L).

21. Hang the dress for twenty-four hours to allow the skirt's bias to stretch, then mark the hem, measuring up from the floor (see page 55). Trim the hem so that it is even, if necessary, and sew a narrow hem (see page 56).

22. To wear the dress, thread the right tie through the left side opening and tie in a bow in the back.

Plaid with Double Pocket

What makes this version special is the fabric, a gorgeous plaid in cocoa and jewel tones. I cut the sash in the same fabric, but on the bias, to add a design accent to the waistline. I also added two large bias-cut pockets layered on top of each other with tied-on button accents, a detail I borrowed directly from a vintage dress I love.

SUPPLIES

- 4 yards (3.7 m) 45"- (114 cm-) or 3½ yards (3.2 m) 60"- (152 cm-) wide fabric
- Thread to match fabric
- ¾ yard (.7 m) 20"- (52 cm-) wide fusible interfacing
- 2 extra-large buttons with large holes

INSTRUCTIONS

1. Cut and construct the dress following steps 1–22 of the Swirl Dress instructions, but cut the ties on the fabric bias (see page 31) (A). All other steps are the same.

2. Create the pockets using the patch pocket piece from the Popover Dress (page 85). Fold down 2" (5 cm) at the top of the pocket pattern and cut two on the fabric bias. Turn each edge

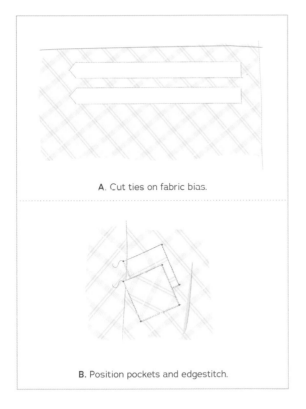

A. Cut ties on fabric bias.

B. Position pockets and edgestitch.

under by 1" (2.5 cm) and stitch to secure, following the instructions on page 62 for creating patch pockets.

3. To place the pockets, try on the dress and pin them to the skirt, overlapping them as desired. Mark the placement and unpin the top pocket. Edgestitch around the bottom pocket to attach it to the skirt (see page 41). Reposition the top pocket and edgestitch (B).

4. Create bias ties for the buttons following the instructions on page 64. Thread the bias ties through the buttons' holes and tie in knots on the front of the buttons. You can leave the ends of the ties cut neatly and they won't fray, since they're on the bias. Place a button on the upper corner of each pocket and hand-stitch them in place, securing the thread through the bias tie at the button's back.

The Boatneck Dress

The Boatneck Dress is a classic vintage silhouette that makes me think of Audrey Hepburn and Grace Kelly. It has a flattering wide bateau neck and a dramatic low-scooped back neckline with a full gathered skirt. This dress includes more intermediate dressmaking skills, including a lapped zipper and a set-in sleeve. The skirt is a gathered rectangle that doesn't require a pattern!

I made this version in the loveliest embroidered cotton, with a decorative scalloped edge that I used on the sleeve hems and skirt hem. Scalloped-edge eyelet would be another fabulous choice for this design. If you'd like to make this in a fabric without a decorative edge, just keep in mind that you'll need to add hem allowances to the sleeves and skirt.

NOTE: Cut one large rectangle for the gathered skirt. It should be your desired length plus a ⅝" (1.5 cm) seam allowance at the waistline and your desired width (this can vary depending on the fullness desired; the skirt pictured is about 3 yards [2.6 m] wide in circumference), plus two seam allowances for the center-back seam, plus a ½" (1.3 cm) hem allowance if you choose to use a fabric without a decorative edge.

SUPPLIES

- 1¼ yards (1.2 m) 45"- (114 cm-) or 1 yard (.9 m) 60"- (152 cm-) wide fabric for bodice plus additional fabric for skirt (see note)
- ½ yard (.5 m) 20"- (51 cm-) wide fusible interfacing
- Thread to match fabric
- 1¼"- (3.2 cm-) wide fusible stay tape or strips of fusible interfacing (see page 34)
- 22"- (56 cm-) long zipper

SKILLS

- Staystitching (page 35)
- Seams (page 39)
- Darts (page 38)
- Neckline facing (page 46)
- Grading and clipping (page 46)
- Understitching (page 47)
- Stitching in the ditch (page 47)
- Set-in sleeve (page 50)
- Gathering (page 41)
- Lapped zipper (page 51)
- Slipstitching (page 57)

PATTERN PIECES

Pattern sheet 4, following layout on page 135.
1. Bodice front (cut 1 on fold, fabric)
2. Bodice back (cut 2, fabric)
3. Front facing (cut 1 on fold, fabric and interfacing)
4. Back facing (cut 2, fabric and interfacing)
5. Sleeve (cut 2, fabric)

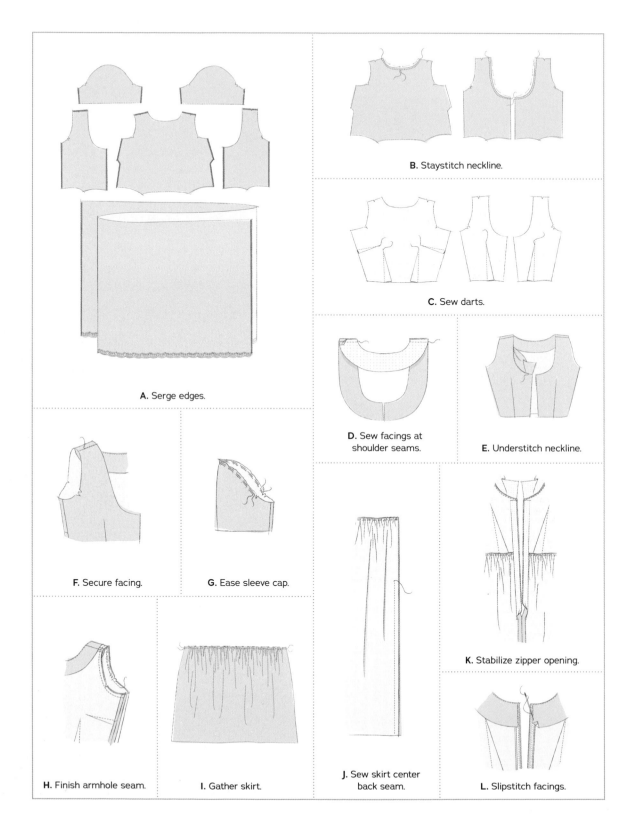

A. Serge edges.

B. Staystitch neckline.

C. Sew darts.

D. Sew facings at shoulder seams.

E. Understitch neckline.

F. Secure facing.

G. Ease sleeve cap.

H. Finish armhole seam.

I. Gather skirt.

J. Sew skirt center back seam.

K. Stabilize zipper opening.

L. Slipstitch facings.

INSTRUCTIONS

1. After cutting the pattern pieces following the layout on page 135, transfer the dart markings and clip into any notches.

2. If you are serge-finishing the raw edges, serge all the vertical seam allowances and the shoulder seam allowances (A).

3. Apply the fusible interfacings to the wrong sides of the corresponding facings, following the instructions on page 34. Finish the lower edges of the front and back facings using the method of your choice (see page 40).

4. Staystitch the neckline front and back (see page 35) (B).

5. Sew the darts on the bodice front and back (see page 38). Press the bust darts toward the waist and the waistline darts toward center front and center back, respectively (C).

6. Pin the bodice front to the bodice backs at the shoulders and side seams, right sides together. Stitch, and press the seam allowances open.

7. Pin the bodice front facing to the bodice back facings at the shoulder seams, right sides together. Stitch, and press the seam allowances open (D).

8. Pin the facing to the bodice neckline, right sides together. Stitch. Grade the neckline seam allowances, remembering that the bodice seam allowance should be the wider one (see page 46). Clip into the inner curves of the neckline (see page 46).

9. Understitch the facing around the neckline (see page 47) (E).

10. Press the neckline, rolling the understitching to the wrong side of the bodice.

11. Secure the facings at the shoulder seams by stitching in the ditch (see page 47) (F).

12. Pin each sleeve right sides together at the underarm seam and sew. Press seam allowances open.

13. Sew two lines of ease stitching along the curved part of the sleeve cap, between notches (see page 50). Pull up the ease stitching so the sleeve cap is rounded but not gathered (G).

14. Pin the sleeve to the armhole, matching the underarm seam to the bodice side seam and matching the notch at the top of the sleeve to the shoulder seam. Stitch from the wrong side of the bodice. Trim the sleeve seam allowance to ⅜" (1 cm) and finish the seam allowances as one, using the method of your choice (see page 40) (H).

15. Sew gathering stitches along the upper edge of the skirt rectangle (see page 41) and pull up the threads to gather (I).

16. Sew the skirt center-back seam, right sides together, from the hem up to 9" (23 cm) below the waistline. Press seam allowances open (J).

17. Pin the gathered skirt to the bodice at the waistline, right sides together, evenly distributing gathers all the way around. Stitch the waistline seam. Trim waistline seam allowances to ⅜" (1 cm) and finish them as one, using the method of your choice. Press seam allowances toward the bodice.

18. Stabilize the back zipper opening by applying 1¼"- (3.2 cm-) wide strips of fusible stay tape to the wrong sides of the seam allowances on both halves of the zipper opening (K).

19. Insert a lapped zipper, following the instructions on page 51.

20. Turn under the seam allowances on the back neckline facing at the zipper opening and slip-stitch them to the zipper tape on the bodice's wrong side (see page 57) (L).

VARIATION

Sheath in Tweed

This version was inspired by wiggle dresses worn by early '60s bombshells, and it's a great choice for date night or the office. Use the three-quarter-length sleeve pattern and add a cute bow and button detail. The skirt is once again just a rectangle, but a slimmer one that gets folded into pleats that meet the bodice darts.

I sewed this up in a lovely cotton tweed, which has the look of a luxurious wool but not the itch factor—so it doesn't require a lining. This also would be gorgeous in a medium-weight cotton like sateen.

SUPPLIES

- 1¼ yards (1.2 m) 45"- (114 cm-) or 1 yard (.9 m) 60"- (152 cm-) wide fabric for bodice plus additional fabric for skirt (see step 3)
- 1 yard (.9 m) 20"- (52 cm-) wide fusible interfacing
- Thread to match fabric
- 1¼"- (3.2 cm-) wide fusible stay tape or strips of fusible interfacing (see page 34)
- 22"- (56 cm-) long zipper
- Two 1" (2.5 cm) buttons

INSTRUCTIONS

1. Follow steps 1–14 of the Boatneck Dress instructions to complete the bodice, using the three-quarter-length sleeve pattern option.

2. Turn under the sleeve hems by 1" (2.5 cm) and hand-stitch in place.

3. Sew the skirt: Cut a rectangle the width of your full hip circumference measurement, plus 2" (5 cm), and the desired length of the skirt, plus waistline seam allowance and hem allowance. Fold the rectangle in half widthwise and mark the fold as center front. Match the center front of the skirt rectangle to the center front of the bodice (the point between the two bodice darts), right sides together. Then pin the skirt back opening to the bodice back opening. Now you will distribute the excess fabric into front and back pleats. Start by making pleats (a doubled-up fold of fabric) that match the placement and depth of the front and back darts. If there

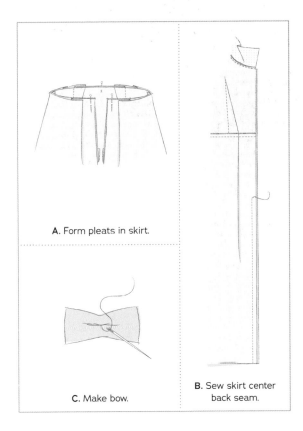

A. Form pleats in skirt.

C. Make bow.

B. Sew skirt center back seam.

right sides together, and sew around the three open sides with a ¼" (6 mm) seam allowance, leaving a 1" (2.5 cm) opening for turning. Trim the corners and turn right side out. Press flat and hand-stitch the opening closed using a slipstitch. Make a small pleat at the center of each rectangle to form a bow and stitch the pleat in place by hand (C). Hand-stitch each bow to the outside of the sleeves at the hems, and then stitch buttons on top of the bows. (I used a kit to cover buttons in my dress fabric, but you can use any button you like.)

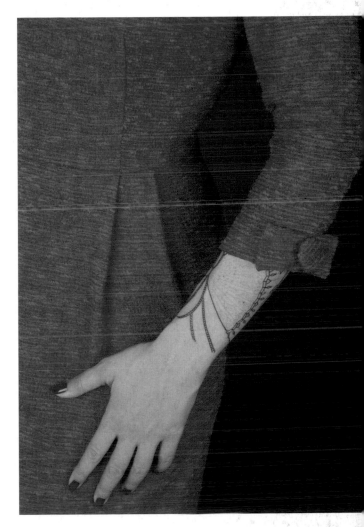

is excess, you can make a second front pleat positioned next to the first pleat, toward the side seam. Pin the skirt in place all the way around and then stitch it to the bodice. Trim and finish the waistline seam allowances and press toward the bodice (A).

4. Sew the skirt center-back seam, right sides together, from the hem up to 9" (23 cm) below the waistline (B).

5. Press the seam allowances open. Hem the skirt with a 1" (2.5 cm) hand-stitched hem, using a slipstitch.

6. Finish the dress following steps 18–20 in the Boatneck Dress instructions.

7. To create the sleeve detail, cut two 4" (10 cm) squares of dress fabric. Fold in half lengthwise,

Party Dress with Flocked Tulle Skirt

This dress shows just how versatile this bodice pattern is. I made it in a double-faced stretch silk (the other side is orange!) and finished the armholes with bias binding. The skirt is two layers: The top layer is a gorgeous hot pink, flocked dot tulle, and the lining layer is a blush pink cotton/silk blend

SUPPLIES

- 1¼ yards (1.2 m) 45"- (114 cm-) or 1 yard (.9 m) 60"- (152 cm-) wide fabric for bodice plus additional fabric for skirt lining (see step 3)
- Thread to match fabric
- 1 yard (.9 m) 20"- (52 cm-) wide fusible interfacing
- 1¼"- (3.2 cm-) wide fusible stay tape or strips of fusible interfacing (see page 34)
- 22"- (56 cm-) long zipper
- Pin-on flower (optional)

INSTRUCTIONS

1. Follow steps 1–11 of the Boatneck Dress instructions to complete the bodice.

2. Measure around an armhole and cut two bias strips (of your main dress fabric) that length plus 1¼" (3.2 cm) for seam allowances. The width of the bias strips should be 1¼" (3.2 cm). Sew the bias strips into a ring using a ⅝" (1.5 cm) seam allowance, and follow the instructions on page 48 to complete the armhole facings. Note that you will sew the facings onto the bodice with a ⅝" (1.5 cm) seam allowance (A, page 124).

3. Cut two rectangles for the skirt layers. The outer layer should be your desired length plus a ⅝" (1.5 cm) waistline seam allowance and your desired width (this can vary depending on the fullness desired; the skirt pictured is about 3 yards [2.6 m] in circumference) plus two ⅝" (1.5 cm) seam allowances for the center-back seam. The lining layer should be the same width and about 1" (2.5 cm) shorter than the outer layer.

4. Sew the center-back seam of each skirt layer separately, right sides together, from the hem up to 9" (23 cm) below the waistline. Press the seam allowances open (B, page 124).

5. Sew a narrow hem on the skirt lining layer (see page 56).

6. Clip into the seam allowances at the base of the zipper opening on both skirt layers. Put the two skirt layers together, both right side out, and baste them together by machine with a long stitch around the waistline and along the zipper opening to secure the layers. Using the clip you made in the back zipper opening seam allowances, turn the seam allowances so that they are both folded to the wrong side of the skirt.

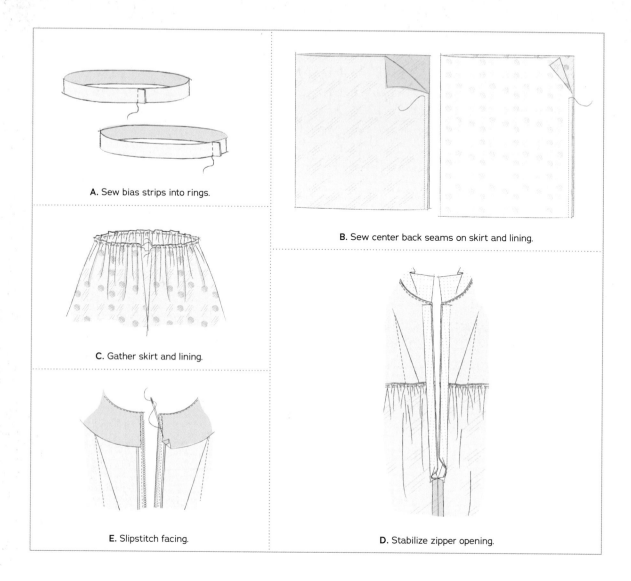

A. Sew bias strips into rings.

B. Sew center back seams on skirt and lining.

C. Gather skirt and lining.

E. Slipstitch facing.

D. Stabilize zipper opening.

7. Sew gathering stitches along the upper edge of the skirt (see page 41) and pull the threads to gather (C).

8. Pin the gathered skirt to the bodice at the waistline, right sides together, evenly distributing the gathers all the way around. Stitch the waistline seam. Trim the seam allowances to ⅜" (1 cm) and finish them as one, using the method of your choice. Press the seam allowances toward the bodice.

9. Stabilize the back zipper opening by applying 1¼"- (3.2 cm-) wide strips of fusible stay tape to the wrong side of the seam allowances on both halves of the zipper opening (D).

10. Insert a lapped zipper, following the instructions on page 51.

11. Turn under the facing's center-back seam allowances at the zipper opening and slipstitch them to the zipper tape (E).

Inside view of Party Dress with Flocked Tulle Skirt

The Patio Dress

This is one of those fabulous styles from the '50s that I've always wanted to re-create in a pattern. Patio dresses (or separates) were western-inspired designs with lots of rickrack trim and ruffly, tiered skirts, and they were souvenir items in the Southwest, as well as popular square-dancing garb. This dress—with its winged collar, cut-on kimono sleeves in either three-quarter or short lengths, and three-tiered skirt—is the epitome of patio dress chic. The best part is picking out your trims. Go crazy with rickrack, pompoms, fringe, and ribbon in all your favorite colors!

For this first dress, I used a crinkly cotton gauze in basic black, the perfect backdrop for some extra flamboyant trims. Skillwise, this dress has you inserting a zipper and sewing a collar. Because of the way this type of vintage collar is constructed, there are some slightly tricky moments sewing the neckline, but I know you can do it! Note that the zipper starts mid-back, because the open neckline makes it easy to get the dress over your head and the zipper positioning keeps the back neckline neat. The skirt is made with long pieces of fabric that are ruffled or gathered, no pattern pieces needed!

This dress is best in lightweight cotton like gauze, batiste, voile, or shirting, or in linen wovens.

SUPPLIES

- 1¾ yards (1.6 m) 45"- (114 cm-) or 60"- (152 cm-) wide fabric for bodice plus several additional yards for skirt (see step 18)
- 1¼ yards (1.2 m) 20"- (52 cm-) wide fusible interfacing
- Thread to match fabric
- A variety of trims (about 1 yard [0.9 m] of each trim for the neckline, and 5 yards [4.6 m] of each for the skirt)
- 1¼"- (3.2 cm-) wide fusible stay tape (see page 51) or strips of fusible interfacing
- 22"- (56 cm-) long zipper

SKILLS

- Neckline facing (page 46)
- Seams (page 39)
- Pivoting (page 39)
- Grading and clipping (page 46)
- Darts (page 38)
- Stitching in the ditch (page 47)
- Staystitching (page 35)
- Understitching (page 47)
- Slipstitching (page 57)
- Topstitch (page 41)
- Gathering (page 41)
- Lapped zipper (page 51)
- Narrow hem (page 56)

PATTERN PIECES

Pattern sheet 5, following layout on page 136.
1. Bodice front (cut 2, fabric)
2. Bodice back (cut 2, fabric)
3. Front facing (cut 2, fabric and interfacing)
4. Back facing (cut 2 on fold, fabric and interfacing)
5. Sleeve facing (cut 2, fabric and interfacing)

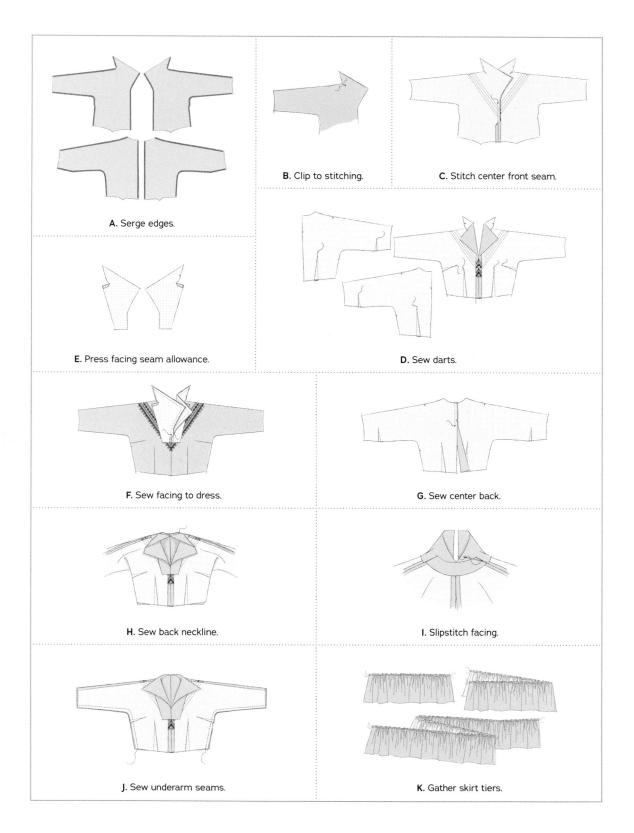

A. Serge edges.

B. Clip to stitching.

C. Stitch center front seam.

E. Press facing seam allowance.

D. Sew darts.

F. Sew facing to dress.

G. Sew center back.

H. Sew back neckline.

I. Slipstitch facing.

J. Sew underarm seams.

K. Gather skirt tiers.

INSTRUCTIONS

1. After cutting the pattern pieces following the layout on page 136, transfer markings (darts, circles, and trim placement lines) and clip into any notches.

2. If you are serge-finishing the raw edges, serge all the vertical seam allowances and the sleeve seam allowances (A).

3. Apply the fusible interfacing to the wrong side of the corresponding facings, following the instructions on page 34.

4. Reinforce the neckline on the bodice front by stitching on the 5⁄8" (1.5 cm) lines,

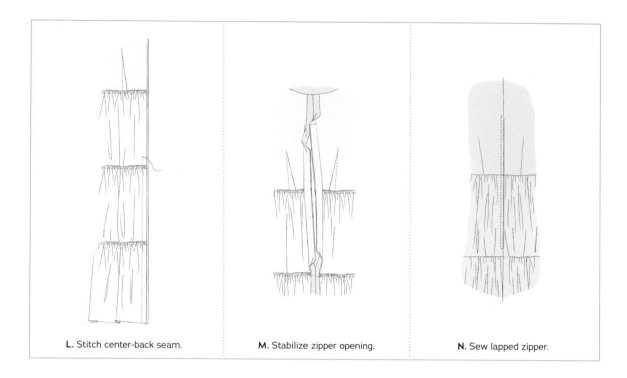

L. Stitch center-back seam.　　**M.** Stabilize zipper opening.　　**N.** Sew lapped zipper.

and pivoting at the inner corner (see page 39). Clip to the stitching at the pivot point (see page 46) (B).

5. Pin and stitch rickrack or other trim along the front trim placement lines. Place each additional row of trim ¼" (6 mm) apart and stitch as many lines as desired.

6. Stitch the bodice center-front seam, stopping at the circle mark and matching trim lines so that they meet in a chevron at the center front. Press the seam allowances open (C).

7. Stich the darts in the bodice front and back and the sleeve backs. Press the waist darts toward center front and the bust darts toward the waist. Press the sleeve darts toward the hem (D).

8. Repeat reinforcement stitching and clipping on the front facings. Turn under the facing's shoulder edge by ⅝" (1.5 cm), as shown, and press (E).

9. Join the front facings at the center-front seam, right sides together, stitching from the lower edge up to the circle marking. Press

the seam allowances open. Finish the lower edge and straight side of the facing as desired.

10. Stitch the front facings to the bodice front, right sides together, starting at the center-back point of the collar and ending at the center-front circle. You will need to stop stitching at the circle where the seam allowances meet and backstitch, then begin stitching again up the opposite side of the front facing. Be sure to keep the other seam allowances out of the way, as this is a tricky joining spot (F).

11. Clip the bodice seam allowances only (not facing) to the circles at the join. Trim down the seam allowances on points and turn the facing to the wrong side of the bodice. Press flat. Stitch in the ditch at the center-front seam to secure the facing in place (see page 47).

12. Staystitch the back necklines (see page 35). With the bodice backs right sides together, stitch the center-back seam from the neckline to the top zipper circle only, backstitching at the circle (G).

13. Stitch front to back at the shoulder and sleeve outer arm seams. Press the seam allowances open.

14. Stitch the back edges of the collar to the back neckline, overlapping the points within the seam allowances at center back (H).

15. Pin back the neckline facing to the back neckline, right sides together, with the collar's back edges sandwiched between the layers, and stitch. Grade the seam allowances and clip into the curves (see page 46). Understitch the facing (see page 47). Turn the facing to the wrong side of the dress and pin it in place at the shoulder seam so that the front facing overlaps the back facing, with the front facing's shoulder seam allowance pressed under. Slipstitch the two facings in place at the shoulder seam (see page 57). Stitch in the ditch of the center-back seam to secure the back facing (I).

16. Sew the bodice front to the bodice back at the side seams, including the sleeves, from the bodice waist to the sleeve openings. Clip into the underarm curves and press the seam allowances open (J).

17. Turn under the sleeve hems 1" (2.5 cm) and topstitch (see page 41) or hand-stitch in place.

18. To calculate the length of each skirt tier, decide how long you want the finished skirt to be and divide that number by three (for the number of tiers). My skirt is 27" (69 cm) long, so each tier is 9" (23 cm) finished. Add seam allowances for the top and bottom of each tier; for example, a 5⁄8" (1.5 cm) seam allowance times 2 equals 1 1⁄4" (3.2 cm), so each of the panels for my tiers needed to be 10 1⁄4" (26 cm) long. Each tier should be about double the circumference of the one above it so that the skirt flares out beautifully. An easy way to figure this out is to make the upper tier twice the circumference of your waist, the middle tier double that, and then the lower tier double that. You will most likely need to seam long pieces together to achieve the necessary tier circumferences, but the seams will not show once everything is gathered (K).

19. Gather the top edge of the upper tier (see page 41) and pin it to the bodice waistline, distributing the gathers evenly. Stitch, leaving the center-back skirt seam unsewn. Finish the waistline seam allowance and press it toward the bodice. Repeat for the middle and lower tiers. Stitch two rows of rickrack just above each skirt tier.

20. Stitch the skirt center-back seam from the hem to 9" (23 cm) below the waistline (L).

21. Stabilize the back zipper opening by fusing 1 1⁄4"- (3.2 cm-) wide strips of fusible stay tape to the wrong sides of the seam allowances on both halves of the zipper opening (M).

22. Sew a lapped zipper, following the instructions on page 51. Stitch a horizontal L-shape at the top and bottom of the zipper (N).

23. Sew a narrow hem on the lower skirt tier (see page 56).

VARIATION

Short-Sleeve Day Dress

The only thing difference with this version is shorter sleeves and no trim.. You can see how this design becomes a versatile day dress when made in a floral. You could also omit the tiers on the skirt and just make a simple skirt (as for the Boatneck Dress on page 112).

SUPPLIES

- 1³⁄₈ yards (1.3 m) 45"- (114 cm-) or 1¹⁄₈ yards (.9 m) 60"- (152 cm-) wide fabric for bodice plus several additional yards for skirt (see step 18)
- ⁷⁄₈ yard (.8 m) 20"- (52 cm-) wide fusible interfacing
- Thread to match fabric
- 1¹⁄₄"- (3.2 cm-) wide fusible stay tape or strips of fusible interfacing (see page 34)
- 22"- (56 cm-) long zipper

PATTERN PIECES

1. Bodice front (cut 2, fabric)
2. Bodice back (cut 2, fabric)
3. Front facing (cut 2, fabric and interfacing)
4. Back facing (cut 2, fabric and interfacing)
5. Sleeve facing (cut 2, fabric and interfacing)

INSTRUCTIONS

1. Follow steps 1–16 of the Patio Dress instructions, cutting the short-sleeve option and omitting any trim.

2. At step 17, instead of hemming the sleeves, apply a sleeve facing, following the instructions on page 46. Cut sleeve facings from fabric and fusible interfacing. Apply the fusible interfacing to the sleeve facings' wrong sides. Form the facings into rings by stitching the short ends right sides together (A). Press the seam allowances open. Pin the sleeve facings to the sleeve openings, right sides together. Stitch. Grade and clip the seam allowances (see page 46), and understitch the facings (see page 47). Turn the sleeve facings to the wrong side and stitch the raw edges in place by hand (B).

3. Complete the skirt following steps 18–23 of the Patio Dress instructions, omitting the trims.

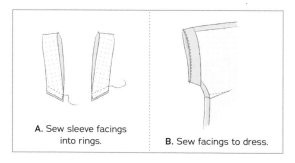

A. Sew sleeve facings into rings.

B. Sew facings to dress.

Pattern Maps

THE POPOVER DRESS

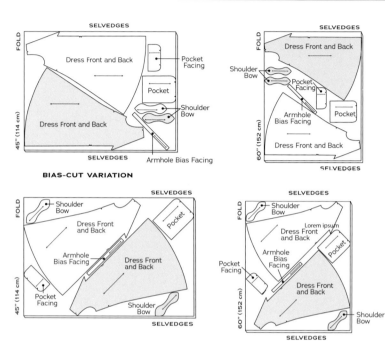

BIAS-CUT VARIATION

THE CHEMISE DRESS

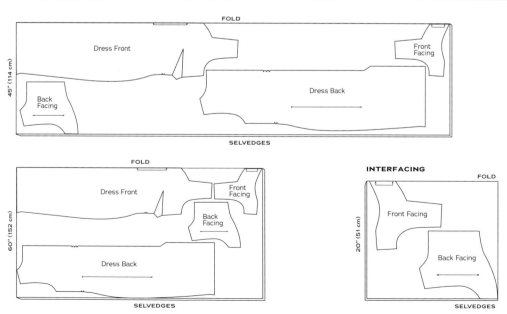

THE SWIRL DRESS

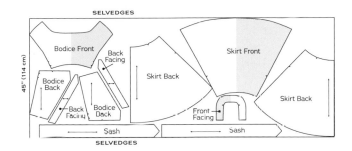

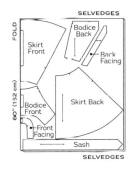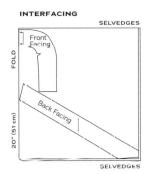

THE BOATNECK DRESS

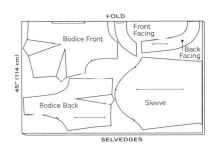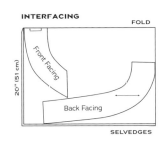

SHORT SLEEVE

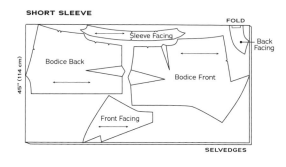

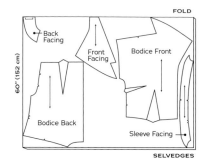

LONG SLEEVE

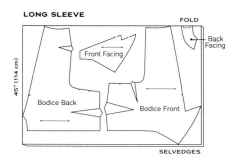

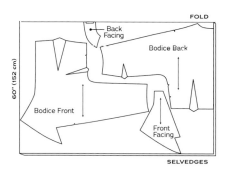

INTERFACING

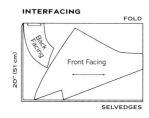

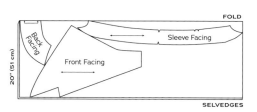

Finished Garment Measurements

THE POPOVER DRESS

	2	4	6	8	10	12	14	16
Bust	40.5" 102.9 cm	42.5" 108 cm	44.5" 113 cm	46.5" 118.1 cm	48.5" 123.2 cm	50.5" 128.2 cm	52.5" 133.4 cm	54.5" 138.4 cm
Waist	49.5" 125.7 cm	51.5" 130.8 cm	53.5" 135.9 cm	55.5" 141 cm	57.5" 146.1 cm	59.5" 151.3 cm	61.5" 156.2 cm	63.5" 161.2 cm
Hips	63" 160 cm	65" 165.1 cm	67" 170.2 cm	69" 175.2 cm	71" 180.3 cm	73" 185.4 cm	75" 190.5 cm	77" 195.6 cm

THE CHEMISE DRESS

	2	4	6	8	10	12	14	16
Bust	35" 89 cm	37" 94 cm	39" 99 cm	41" 104.1 cm	43" 109.2 cm	45" 114.3 cm	47" 119.4 cm	49" 124.5 cm
Waist	35.5" 90.2 cm	37.5" 95.3 cm	39.5" 100.3 cm	41.5" 105.4 cm	43.5" 110.5 cm	45.5" 115.6 cm	47.5" 120.6 cm	49.5" 125.7 cm
Hips	39.5" 100.3 cm	41.5" 105.4 cm	43.5" 110.5 cm	45.5" 115.6 cm	47.5" 120.7 cm	49.5" 125.7 cm	51.5" 130.8 cm	53.5" 135.9 cm

THE SWIRL DRESS

	2	4	6	8	10	12	14	16
Bust	37" 94 cm	39" 99 cm	41" 104.1 cm	43" 109.2 cm	45" 114.3 cm	47" 119.4 cm	49" 124.5 cm	51" 129.5 cm
Waist	25" 63.5 cm	27" 68.6 cm	29" 73.7 cm	31" 78.7 cm	33" 83.8 cm	35" 88.9 cm	37" 94 cm	39" 99.1 cm
Hips	50" 127 cm	52" 132.1 cm	54" 137.1 cm	56" 142.2 cm	58" 147.3 cm	60" 152.4 cm	62" 157.5 cm	64" 162.6 cm

THE BOATNECK DRESS

	2	4	6	8	10	12	14	16
Bust	33.5" 85 cm	35.5" 90 cm	37.5" 95.3 cm	39.5" 100.3 cm	41.5" 105.4 cm	43.5" 110.5 cm	45.5" 155.6 cm	47.5" 120.6 cm
Waist	24.375" 61.9 cm	26.375" 67 cm	28.375" 72 cm	30.375" 77.1 cm	32.375" 82.2 cm	34.375" 87.3 cm	36.375" 92.4 cm	38.375" 97.5 cm

THE PATIO DRESS

	2	4	6	8	10	12	14	16
Bust	35.75" 90.8 cm	37.75" 95.9 cm	39.75" 101 cm	41.75" 106 cm	43.75" 111.1 cm	45.75" 116.2 cm	47.75" 121.2 cm	49.75" 126.4 cm
Waist	24.5" 62.2 cm	26.5" 67.3 cm	28.5" 72.4 cm	30.5" 77.5 cm	32.5" 82.6 cm	34.5" 87.6 cm	36.5" 92.7 cm	38.5" 97.8 cm

Resources

Here are some of my favorite resources for sewing supplies, as well as some recommendations for further reading.

B&J Fabrics
www.bandjfabrics.com
Most of the projects in this book were made with fabrics provided by B&J Fabrics. You can purchase them in person at their store (525 Seventh Ave., New York, NY 10018; 2nd floor; 212-354-8150) or online.

By Gertie
www.bygertie.com
This is my site, where you can purchase my fabrics and patterns, take my online courses, and read my blog!

Fashion Sewing Supply
www.fashionsewingsupply.com
My favorite interfacing source.

Malco Modes
www.malcomodes.biz
My favorite source for affordable petticoats to give your dresses that vintage look.

SewKeysE by Emma Seabrooke
www.shop.emmaseabrooke.com
Sells a wide variety of fusible stay tapes, great for quickly stabilizing zipper openings and necklines.

Sew True
www.sewtrue.com
A great source for patternmaking supplies, such as paper, rulers, and French curves.

What Katie Did
www.whatkatiedid.com
This site sells merry widows, longline bras, waist cinchers, and other beautiful vintage-inspired lingerie for an era-appropriate silhouette.

RECOMMENDED READING

Couture Sewing Techniques
by Claire B. Schaeffer

Design Your Own Dress Patterns
by Adele P. Margolis

Fit for Real People
by Patti Palmer and Maria Alto

Patternmaking for Fashion Design
by Helen Joseph Armstrong

Reader's Digest Complete Guide to Sewing
by Reader's Digest

Threads magazine

Acknowledgments

It's hard to believe that this is my fifth book! I owe immense gratitude to everyone who has followed me over the years; thank you for sticking with me through more than a decade of darts and dresses.

Thank you to Shawna Mullen and Meredith Clark at Abrams for making this book a reality. Stephani Miller provided excellent technical editing, and designer Susi Oberhelman made everything look gorgeous, even those pesky pattern sheets!

I brought in my Charm Patterns (www.charmpatterns.bygertie.com) team for the illustrations and photos, and they nailed it, as usual. Gemini H did the lovely color illustrations, and Robin Kataja-Blair is a wizard with technical illustrations.

I cannot thank my photo "dream team" enough for helping me fulfill my vintage glamour vision: Sophie Spinelle and Angela Altus of Shameless Photography and Melissa Firestone of Hairstyling by Melissa, who did my hair and makeup to perfection.

Thank you to Alyson Clair, who did the pattern grading, and to Katie Knight, my assistant while working on the dresses for this book.

B&J Fabrics provided the gorgeous fabric for the book. I'd like to thank Scott and the whole team there for being incredibly supportive of me over the years, as well as providing a lovely place to shop for fabric (you must go if you're ever in New York!). Visit www.bandjfabrics.com for more information.

Thank you to my mom, Patty Sauer, for the encouragement over the years, and to my furry little sewing companions, Hattie and Henry.

Index

About the Author

Gretchen "Gertie" Hirsch is a sewing writer and designer with a passion for vintage glamour and quality dressmaking. She's the author of *Gertie's Ultimate Dress Book, Gertie Sews Vintage Casual, Gertie's New Book for Better Sewing,* and *Gertie's New Fashion Sketchbook.* She started a popular blog on vintage sewing more than ten years ago and now has a bustling business writing books and designing fabric and patterns. She has her own pattern line with Butterick and Simplicity, as well as her own independently published Charm Patterns by Gertie. She also designs fabric for Fabric Traditions and Michael Miller Fabrics. She travels the world teaching sewing workshops on her time-tested techniques for fitting and beautiful dressmaking. Visit her online at www.bygertie.com.

The Patio Dress (page 127)

TO ALL MY FELLOW SEWISTS, PAST AND PRESENT

Editor: Meredith A. Clark
Designer: Susi Oberhelman
Production Manager: Kathleen Gaffney

Library of Congress Control Number: 2017956801

ISBN: 978-1-4197-3234-8
eISBN: 978-1-68335-322-5

Printed and bound in China
10 9 8 7 6 5 4 3 2 1

ABRAMS The Art of Books
195 Broadway, New York, NY 10007
abramsbooks.com